高等学校英语专业系列教材
Textbook Series for Tertiary English Majors

高等学校英语专业系列教材 求知 STEM
Textbook Series for Tertiary English Majors

总 主 编 石 坚

副总主编 黄国文 陈建平 张绍杰 蒋洪新

编委单位（排名不分先后）

广东外语外贸大学	华南农业大学
广西大学	陕西师范大学
云南大学	武汉大学
中山大学	贵州大学
中南大学	贵州师范大学
四川大学	重庆大学
东北师范大学	重庆邮电大学
西安外国语大学	湖南师范大学
西安交通大学	……
华中师范大学	

策 划 张鸽盛 饶邦华 周小群

高等学校英语专业系列教材
Textbook Series for Tertiary English Majors

STEM | 求知

总 主 编：石 坚
副总主编：黄国文 陈建平 张绍杰 蒋洪新

中国文化概论
（第3版）

A An Introduction to Chinese Culture

✛ 主编 周 仪 廖建思

重庆大学出版社

内容提要

本书主要针对我国英语专业学生对祖国传统文化不甚了解，或者即使了解一些但却不知道如何用英语表达的情况而编写。本书旨在让学生既学习英语语言知识，又学习中国文化知识。全书共7章，涉及中国历史、中国文化传统、文学与艺术、科学技术、教育、传统习俗、旅游文化等方面。本书可作为英语专业学生的教材使用，也可供其他具有相当英语水平的学习者使用。

图书在版编目（CIP）数据

中国文化概论：英文 / 周仪，廖建思主编. -- 3版

. -- 重庆：重庆大学出版社，2019.3（2023.7重印）

求知高等学校英语专业系列教材

ISBN 978-7-5689-1452-9

Ⅰ.①中… Ⅱ.①周… ②廖… Ⅲ.①英语—高等学

校—教材②中华文化 Ⅳ.①H319.39

中国版本图书馆CIP数据核字（2018）第298323号

中国文化概论（第3版）

周 仪 廖建思 主 编

责任编辑：杨 琪 版式设计：叶抒扬

责任校对：王 倩 责任印制：赵 晟

*

重庆大学出版社出版发行

出版人：饶帮华

社址：重庆市沙坪坝区大学城西路21号

邮编：401331

电话：（023）88617190 88617185（中小学）

传真：（023）88617186 88617166

网址：http://www.cqup.com.cn

邮箱：fxk@cqup.com.cn（营销中心）

全国新华书店经销

重庆亘鑫印务有限公司印刷

*

开本：787mm×1092mm 1/16 印张：11.5 字数：251千

2019年3月第3版 2023年7月第16次印刷

ISBN 978-7-5689-1452-9 定价：39.00元

总　序

　　进入 21 世纪，高等教育呈现快速扩展的趋势。我国高等教育从外延式发展过渡到内涵式发展后，"质量"已成为教育改革与发展的关键词。由国务院颁布的《国家中长期教育改革和发展规划纲要（2010—2020）》（以下简称《纲要》）明确要求狠抓本科教育人才培养存在的主要问题，厘清高等教育人才培养目标、理念、社会需求，制订本科教学培养模式、教学内容和方法、质量保障与评估机制，切实提高人才培养的质量。我国英语专业在过去的数十年中经过几代人的努力，取得了显著的成绩和长足的发展。特别是近年来随着经济社会的快速发展和对外交流活动的增多，"一带一路"　　　的提出和"讲好中国故事"的需要，英语专业的学科地位也随之大大提升，其　　　　　　十分庞大。英语专业虽然经历了一个"跨越式""超常规"的发展历　　　　　　　　培养质量下滑、专业建设和人才需求出现矛盾、毕业生就业　　　　　　　　，英语专业的教育、教学与育人又到了一个不得不改的关键　

　　《纲要》在强调狠抓培养质量的同时，也提出了培　　　　　　、通晓国际规则、能参与国际事务和国际竞争"人才的战略方针。基于这样　　　，外语专业教学指导委员会明确提出了人才"多元培养，分类卓越"的理念。基于这　　的理念，即将颁布的《英语专业本科教学质量国家标准》（以下简称《国标》）对英语专业本科的现有课程设置提出新的改革思路：英语专业课程体系包括公共课程、专业核心课程、专业方向课程、实践环节和毕业论文（设计）五个部分；逐步压缩英语技能课程，用"内容依托式"课程替代传统的英语技能课程，系统建设语言学、文学、文化、国别研究等方面的专业课程。

　　自 2001 年开始，在重庆大学出版社的大力支持下，我们成立了由华中、华南、西南和西北以及东北地区的知名专家、学者和教学一线教师组成的"求知高等学校英语专业系列教材"编写组，以《高等学校英语专业英语教学大纲》为依据，将社会的需求与培养外语人才的全面发展紧密结合，注重英语作为一个专业的学科系统性和科学性，注重英语教学和习得的方法与规律，培养学生能力和育人并举，突出特色和系列教材的内在逻辑关系，反映了教学改革的新理念并具有前瞻性，建立了与英语专业课程配套的新教材体系。"求知高等学校英语专业系列教材"经历了 10 余年教学实践的锤炼，通过不断的修订来契合教学的发展变化，在教材的整体性和开放性、学生基本技能和实际应用能力的培养、学生的人文素质和跨文化意识的培养这三方面上有所突破。通过这套系列教材的开发建设工作，我们一直在探讨新的教学理念、模式，探索英语专业人才培养的新路子。今天，我们以《国

标》为依据，回顾我们过去十多年在教学改革上所做的努力，我们欣慰地看到我们的方向是契合英语专业学科定位和发展的。随着《国标》指导思想的明确，为了适应英语专业学科课程设置的进一步调整，我们对"求知高等学校英语专业系列教材"进行了最新一轮的建设工作。

全新的系列教材力求在以下方面有所创新：

第一，围绕听、说、读、写、译五种能力的培养来构建教材体系。在教材内容的总体设置上，颠覆以往"以课程定教材"的观念，不再让教材受制于刻板的课程设置体系，而是引入 Program 理念，根据《国标》中对学生的能力要求，针对某方面的具体能力编写对应的系列教材。读写和听说系列不再按照难度区分混合编排题材，而是依据文体或专业性质的自然划分，分门别类地专册呈现，便于教师在教学中根据实际需要搭配组合使用。例如，阅读教材分为小说类、散文类、新闻类等；口语教材按专题成册，分为基本表述、演讲、辩论等。

第二，将五种能力的提升融入人文素养的综合提升之中。坚持英语专业教育的人文本位，强调文化熏陶。在跨学科新专业不断涌现的背景下，盲目追求为每种新专业都专门编写一套教材，费时费力。最佳的做法是坚持英语专业核心教材的人文性，培养学生优秀的语言文化素养，并在此基础上依照专业要求填补相关知识上的空缺，形成新的教材配比模式和体系。

第三，以"3E"作为衡量教材质量的标准。教材的编写上，体现 Engaging, Enabling, Enlightening 的"3E"功能，强调教材的人文性与语言文化综合能力的培养，淡化技能解说。

第四，加入"微课""翻转课堂"等元素，便于课堂互动的开展。创新板块、活动的设计，相对减少灌输式的 lecture，增加学生参与的 seminar。

我们希望通过对这套系列教材的全新修订和建设，落实《国标》精神，继续推动高等学校英语专业教学改革，为提高英语专业人才的培养质量探索新的实践方法，为英语专业的学生拓展求知的新空间。

"求知高等学校英语专业系列教材"编委会

2017 年 6 月

Preface

At the beginning of the 1990s, when the first group of American students came to study at Guangxi University, I was assigned to teach them Chinese culture. They were interested in this course very much. Having learned something about Confucianism and Taoism, they had a discussion with our students in the English Department. I was shocked to find how little our students know about our own ancestors. They were so ignorant of our history and our national heritage that some of them had no idea which historical period Confucius lived in or what his famous sayings were, and many of them dared not utter a word throughout the discussion.

This reminded me of what Chairman Mao said in his article *Reform Our Study:*

> Many party members are still in a fog about Chinese history, whether of the last hundred years or of ancient times. There are many Marxist Leninist scholars who cannot open their mouths without citing ancient Greece; but as for their own ancester—sorry, they have been forgotten.

It occurred to me that it might benefit our students (both Chinese and American) if they had a textbook on Chinese culture written in English. I talked it over with Prof. Liang Yihua, who was then Director for International Relations of Guangxi University. He shared my idea. With our collaborative effort, *Chinese Culture* came out in 1994. The book, however, limited in space, deals only with Chinese cultural traditions—Confucianism, Taoism and Buddhism. We have been longing to rewrite it, and expand it so that our students will be provided with more, extensive information covering every aspect of Chinese culture.

Thanks to the editors of Chongqing University Press who are organizing scholars from the universities in Northwest, Southwest and Central China to compile a series of textbooks for the English majors, including *An Introduction to Chinese Culture*, which I volunteer to undertake.

This book is based upon my previous books on Chinese culture and my experience in teaching this course for the past ten years. After six months of intense work, I now have a pile of finished manuscripts on my desk and some breathing space.

My acknowledgements should go to those authors whose works I have consulted. I especially would like to thank my dear friend and colleague Professor Liang Yihua and American teacher Pattricia Ann Cobb and British teacher Cheritan Hunt, who helped to read the manuscripts chapter by chapter and gave me many suggestions.

Zhou Yi

Guangxi University

March, 2003

修订说明

2017 年新年伊始，中共中央办公厅、国务院办公厅印发了《关于实施中华优秀传统文化传承发展工程的意见》（以下简称《意见》）。《意见》指出："文化是民族的血脉，是人民的精神家园。文化自信是更基本、更深层、更持久的力量。中国文化独一无二的理念、智慧、气质、神韵，增添了中国人民和中华民族内心深处的自信和自豪。""中华文化源远流长、灿烂辉煌。在 5000 多年文化发展中孕育的中华优秀传统文化，积淀着中华民族最深沉的精神追求，代表着中华民族独特的精神标识，是中华民族生生不息、发展壮大的丰厚滋养，是中国特色社会主义植根的文化沃土，是当代中国发展的突出优势，对延续和发展中华文明、促进人类文明进步，发挥着重要的作用。""实施中华优秀文化传承工程，是建设社会主义文化强国的重大战略任务，对于传承中华文脉、全面提高人民群众文化素质、维护国家的治理体系和治理能力现代化，具有重要意义。"

本书的修订以《意见》的精神为指导，用英语全面地介绍中华优秀传统文化，使我们的大学生在传统文化的熏陶下，具备"良好行为规范，高雅审美情趣，质朴道德操守、深邃哲学思想"，在未来的涉外活动中，不卑不亢、谦和自信，弘扬和传承中华优秀传统文化。

本书的修订目标是：保持本书的经典性、人文性和知识性，培养学生优秀的语言文化素质；使我们的大学生具有深厚的文化底蕴，对祖国的文化精髓，能用英语如数家珍般说出来。

考虑到此书已被广大读者接受、被全国多所大学采用为教材，本书在修订中力图保持它原有的趣味性，使我们的学生发觉学习中华传统文化是十分有趣的事情，而用英语来表达深奥的古文并不是一件难事。

本书的修订增加了课堂互动的教学设计，如课堂讨论（seminar）、课堂展示（presentation）、问答、背诵古典诗词等，以培养学生的口语能力。

本书尽量用简易英语（easy English）写作，删除了原书中一些难懂的哲学讲解，并对必要的经典陈述附上中文。通过修订，我们希望本书成为讲述中国文化通识知识的英文教材。

编　者
2018 年 9 月

Contents

Chapter One

Chinese History

- A Chronological Table of Chinese History
- A Brief Account of Chinese History

I
A Chronological Table of Chinese History
（中国历史编年表）

Dynasty（朝代）	Era（纪元）
the Five Emperors	3000 B.C.E.—2100 B.C.E.
Xia Dynasty（夏）	2100 B.C.E.—1600 B.C.E.
Shang Dynasty（商）	1600 B.C.E.—1100 B.C.E.
Zhou Dynasty（周）	Western Zhou Dynasty（西周）1100 B.C.E.—771 B.C.E.
	Eastern Zhou Dynasty（东周）770 B.C.E.—256 B.C.E.
Qin Dynasty（秦）	221 B.C.E.—206 B.C.E.
Han Dynasty（汉）	Western Han（西汉）206 B.C.E.—25 A.D.
	Eastern Han（东汉）25 A.D.—220 A.D.
Three Kingdoms（三国）	Wei（魏）220 A.D.—265 A.D.
	Shu Han（蜀汉）221 A.D.—263 A.D.
	Wu（吴）222 A.D.—280 A.D.
Western Jin Dynasty（西晋）	265 A.D.—317 A.D.
Eastern Jin Dynasty（东晋）	317 A.D.—420 A.D.
Southern Dynasties（南朝）	Song（宋）420 A.D.—479 A.D.
	Qi（齐）479 A.D.—502 A.D.
	Liang（梁）502 A.D.—557 A.D.
	Chen（陈）557 A.D.—589 A.D.
Northern Dynasties（北朝）	Northern Wei（北魏）386 A.D.—534 A.D.
	Eastern Wei（东魏）534 A.D.—550 A.D.
	Northern Qi（北齐）550 A.D.—577 A.D.
	Western Wei（西魏）535 A.D.—556 A.D.
	Nothern Zhou（北周）557 A.D.—581 A.D.
Sui Dynasty（隋）	581 A.D.—618 A.D.
Tang Dynasty（唐）	618 A.D.—907 A.D.
Five Dynasties（五代）	Later Liang（后梁）907 A.D.—923 A.D.
	Later Tang（后唐）923 A.D.—936 A.D.
	Later Jin（后晋）936 A.D.—947 A.D.
	Later Han（后汉）947 A.D.—950 A.D.
	Later Zhou（后周）951 A.D.—960 A.D.
Song Dynasty（宋）	Northern Song Dynasty（北宋）960 A.D.—1127 A.D.
	Southern Song Dynasty（南宋）1127 A.D.—1279 A.D.

Continued

Dynasty（朝代）	Era（纪元）
Liao Dynasty（辽）	907 A.D.—1125 A.D.
Jin Dynasty（金）	1115 A.D.—1234 A.D.
Yuan Dynasty（元）	1206 A.D.—1368 A.D.
Ming Dynasty（明）	1368 A.D.—1644 A.D.
Qing Dynasty（清）	1616 A.D.—1911 A.D.
Republic of China（中华民国）	1912 A.D.—1949 A.D.
People's Republic of China（中华人民共和国）	1949 A.D.—

·*Exercise*·

Sum up the chronological table of Chinese history in one sentence.

II

A Brief Account of Chinese History

China is a large country with a long history. It has a territory about the size of Europe and a population about a quarter of that of the world. In this vast country of ours, there are large areas of fertile land which provide us with food and clothing; mountain ranges which are covered with forests and abound in mineral deposits; rivers and lakes which furnish us with water transport and irrigation; a long coastline which facilitates communication with nations beyond the seas. From ancient times our forefathers have labored, lived and multiplied on this vast territory.

China is one of the four homes of the world's earliest civilizations. It has a recorded history of nearly 4,000 years. Throughout the history of Chinese civilization its agriculture and handicrafts have been renowned for their high level of sophistication. During these 4,000 years, China has nurtured many great thinkers, scientists, inventors, statesmen, strategists, men of letters and artists, yielding a rich cultural heritage and fine cultural traditions.

The ancient civilization of China has exercised great influence on the modern world. Ezra Pound's translation of Confucian philosophy aroused great interest from the Western world in Eastern philosophy, and his translation of many ancient Chinese poems interested men of letters in the West. The personal dinner place settings used by the first three American presidents, George Washington, John Adams and Thomas Jefferson, were of Chinese origin, a vivid evidence of China's artistic attraction for the American founding fathers.

The Chinese history can be divided into two periods: the ancient period (ancient times—1840) and the modern period (1840—present).

The Ancient Period

Chinese history began with two legendary figures—Emperor Huang (黄帝) and Emperor Yan (炎帝), who, together with their tribes, inhabited in the area of Huanghe River (the Yellow River) basin in the years around 3000 B.C.E. By the time of Xia Dynasty (夏朝, 2100 B.C.E.—1600 B.C.E.) after centuries of living side by side, these two tribes gradually melted into one. That's why the Chinese people usually call themselves "the descendants of Yan and Huang" (炎黄子孙). People at that time believed that the land they lived on was the center of the world, and called their state the "Middle Kingdom", thus giving China its country name.

Although there are no reliable historical data to test the existence of this period, yet legends are abundant, and modern archaeology has found authentic materials—pottery vessels, stone tools and weapons as offerings to accompany the dead in the unearthed ancient tombs, which provide evidence of the life of our ancestors before the Xia Dynasty.

There are many legends describing the life of the people in this period, especially of the three sage Kings after Emperor Huang and Emperor Yan—Yao (尧), Shun (舜) and Yu (禹). Let's quote some here for you to enjoy.

How Yao and Shun Passed the Throne to the Worthy and the Capable （尧、舜禅让）

According to the *Book of History* (《尚书》, a book of ancient times, recording the history from the time of Yao, Shun, Yu down to the early Zhou Dynasty), when Yao was very old, he summoned the chiefs of the Four Mountains and said, "I have been on the throne for seventy years. Who can carry out the mandate of Heaven in place of me?" The chiefs of the Four Mountains all said, "We have no such virtues. We would only disgrace the throne. Your son is the right person to ascend the throne." Yao said, "I know him, he is mean and stupid." And Yao asked his officials to recommend someone else. Then the King was told that there was a poor young man named Shun. He was the son of a blind man. His father was wicked, his mother deceitful and his brother arrogant, yet he was filial to them and lived with them in harmony. The King said, "That is the right person to be the new king. I will try him. I will wive him with my two daughters, and observe his behavior." So his two daughters, Owang (娥皇) and NuYing (女瑛), came to the bend of the Gui

River to be the wives of Shun. Years later Shun ascended the throne.

As the legend has it, when Shun inspected the southern states, he became very ill and died in Xiang（湘，at present Hunan Province）. His two wives followed his footsteps to Xiang and cried to death. Their tears dented the bamboo, which is the bamboo we have now in Hunan Province, called "tear bamboo"（斑竹）.

How Yu, the Great, Conquered the Flood（大禹治水）

Some time around 2200 B.C.E., a great flood covered the earth. Shun sent Gun（鲧），Yu's father to control the flood. Gun led people to build dams to block the flood but failed. So Shun gave order to kill Gun. When Yu grew up, he undertook his father's unfinished task. This time he drew from the lessons of his father. He did not build dams, but led people to dig ditches to lead the water away. He worked ceaselessly for thirteen years and succeeded in bringing the flood under control. As the legend has it, so busy was he that "thrice he had gone past his own house without even looking in." As a reward for his achievement, Shun passed the throne to Yu. When Yu died, his son Qi（启）seized power and founded Xia, the first dynasty in China, thus beginning the hereditary system in Chinese history.

The Xia Dynasty（夏朝，2100 B.C.E.—1600 B.C.E.）

The ethnic group of the Xia Dynasty is the Hua Xia nationality. That's why the Chinese people are also called the Hua People in other parts of the world.

At the beginning of the Xia Dynasty the Youhu tribe（有扈氏部落）in the west border rose in rebellion. King Qi led his army and defeated the enemy in Gan（甘），at present in Henan Province. This is the first battle recorded in Chinese history.

Farming and stock breeding were already well developed in the Xia Dynasty. People were familiar with the phenomena of the changes of seasons and arranged their farm work and other activities accordingly.

The last king of Xia, Jie（桀），is notorious in Chinese history for his debauchery. He built "ponds of wine and forests of meat"（酒池肉林）to entertain himself and his concubines, resulting in the fall of the state.

One thing worth mentioning is that one of Kings of Xia, Shaokang（少康），used sorghum to brew wine in about 1800 B.C.E., thus began the Chinese culture of wine.

The Shang Dynasty（商朝，1600 B.C.E.—1100 B.C.E.）

The Shang Dynasty is renowned for its high development of bronze techniques which brought about the separation of Chinese society into town and country dwellers. The nobility and their craftsmen lived in towns, supported by the peasants living in the countryside.

Regular religious rites were popular among the Shang nobles. In addition to a supreme god, they worshipped the spirits of their ancestors. The ceremonies involved the sacrifice of hundreds of animals, domestic as well as those obtained from the hunt. Their tombs were filled with hundreds of objects made of gold, jade, bronze and stone, for their use in the after-life, and in many cases, their slaves were buried with them as well.

Our knowledge of the Shang period comes not only from the excavations of ancient tombs, but also from the inscriptions on oracle bones and tortoise shells. In the time of the Shang, a favorite method of divination was to scrape a thin spot on a tortoise shell, put it over a flame, and have diviners interpret the cracks that appeared on the shell. This was the beginning of the Chinese written language.

The dissoluteness and extravagance of the Shang rulers led to the revolt of the people, and the establishment of the Zhou Dynasty.

The Zhou Dynasty （周朝, 1100 B.C.E.—256 B.C.E.）

The Zhou Dynasty lasted for over 800 years, dividing the Western Zhou and Eastern Zhou, which includes the Spring and Autumn and Warring States Periods.

The Zhou Dynasty is a significant period in Chinese history for it saw the evolution of the Chinese society from a slave system to a feudal one. It also witnessed the flourishing of Chinese culture.

It is interesting to note how the Shang Dynasty came to its end. King Zhou（纣王）, the last Shang emperor, was a debauched tyrant. He used to dine with three thousand people in a forest whose leaves were made of meat and they drank like cows from a pond of wine. Meanwhile, the state of Zhou had gained influence among the vassal（封臣的） states because of its wise ruler, Ji Chang（姬昌）, who later became King Wen（文王） of the Zhou Dynasty. Ji Chang's reputation and influence made King Zhou jealous. On one of Ji Chang's tributary（进贡的） visits to the Shang court, King Zhou threw him in prison, where he was confined for seven years. While in prison, Ji Chang reflected on *Yin*（阴） and *Yang*（阳） and had the idea to put Fuxi's（伏羲） trigram upon trigram to form a hexagram, symbolizing a higher level of diversification. He gave names to the sixty-four possible hexagrams and attached to each a text to convey its attribute. Later, the oracle announcements of the hexagrams were annotated and embellished by *Confucius*, and *Ten Wings*（十翼） were attached to it. That is how the book *I-Ching*（《易经》） came down to us.

As the legend has it, Fuxi observed the phenomena in Heaven at night（夜观星象）, studied the developments of things on Earth（日察地理）, learned the languages of birds and animals and the disposition of the land, drew from the lessons of persons near and things afar, and then created the eight trigrams（八卦） which are figures made up of three elements that are either *Yin* or *Yang*, symbolizing Heaven, Earth, Thunder, Water, Mountain, Wind, Fire and Lake.

According to the *Book of History*, King Zhou was surprised to know that Ji Chang had created the hexagrams and could foretell the future with them. So when Ji Chang's son came to visit his imprisoned father, King Zhou killed him, made cakes of his flesh and sent them to Ji Chang to see whether he knew the truth. Ji Chang cast a hexagram and knew it was his son's meat. Would he eat the cakes? If not, King Zhou would kill him; if yes, how could a father eat his own son's meat? After praying to god to pardon him, he swallowed up the meat cake which rolled up and down in his stomach and he felt like vomiting. Then he vomitted out the meat cake which immediately turned into a rabbit and ran away. That's the origin of rabbits on earth.（The English words "vomit" and "rabbit" have the same Chinese sound "tu".）

The release of Ji Chang was eventually arranged by bribing King Zhou with beautiful women, fine horses and rare animals. King Zhou was so pleased with the gifts that he even granted Ji Chang the right to bear arms against his neighboring states.

The plan to overthrow King Zhou was long under way. Ji Chang had taken advantage of the right to bring his immediate neighbors in line. Then he sought out the wise hermit Jiang Shang（姜尚）, known to later ages as the old Master Jiang（姜太公）, to be his right-hand man.

Old Master Jiang spent his time fishing, with a straight hook, thirty inches above water. When asked about this seemingly futile exercise, he answered, "What I am after is not fish, but princes and emperors." That is to say, he eschewed the material glories of the world to wait for the call of a true noble cause.

Ji Chang died without taking actions against King Zhou. His successor, Ji Fa（姬发）, who later became King Wu（武王）, made Jing Shang his Chief-of-Staff. Two years later his call for a revolution was answered by all the neighboring states, which came forth with four thousand chariots. Before the joint forces assembled in the field of Mu（牧野，今河南淇县附近）, he delivered a historic speech that was preserved for posterity in the *Book of History*.

King Zhou met the rebellious forces with an army of seven hundred thousand. However, it was a ragtag army（乌合之众）with no will to fight, and most of the soldiers went over to King Wu. Disaster did befall the evil Zhou. Conceding defeat, he retreated to the Deer Pavilion（鹿台）, scene of his numerous past orgies. There, clasping to his bosom his priceless jade collection, King Zhou burned himself to death. The downfall of the Shang Dynasty heralded a new period in China's history—the Zhou Dynasty.

The Zhou period witnessed the "contention of one hundred schools of thought"（百家争鸣）. Among them the most famous are Confucius（孔子）, Mencius（孟子）, Lao Zi（老子）, Zhuang Zi（庄子）, Mo Zi（墨子） and Han Fei Zi（韩非子）.

Confucius held that through the restoration of the early Zhou's ritual and self-cultivation, a man's conduct would become noble, unselfish, just and benevolent. Mencius believed that man's nature was basically good, while Xun Zi, another Confucian, argued that it was basically evil. Those opposed to Confucius included Mo Zi who preached a doctrine of universal love as the basis for peace and order. The response of the Taoists, however, to the moral and physical upheavals was to favor not strong government, but no government at all. Human institutions, ambition and striving were rejected in favor of simplicity, humanity and a return to nature.

Both the Confucian and Taoist schools were to have an immense influence on later Chinese thought. But the immediate winners in the controversies of the period were the legalists（法家） who held that human nature was essentially evil, and only a system of reward and punishment could ensure the survival of the state and its supremacy over all others.

The Qin Dynasty （秦朝, 221 B.C.E.—206 B.C.E.）

With the help of the political and social reforms carried out by Shang Yang（商鞅）, a legalist, Qin Shihuang（秦始皇）, the First Emperor of the Qin Dynasty, succeeded in annexing the other six states and established the first centralized monarchy in Chinese history.

Though the Qin Dynasty lasted only 15 years, its significance in Chinese history is tremendous. The Qin Empire ushered in four centuries of unity under itself and the succeeding Han Emperors. The country was divided into provinces and districts, all placed under the control of the central government; the written language was simplified and made uniform, and the weights, measures and coinage were standardized. A network of roads was built, stretching from the capital to the furthest limits of the Empire, while standard dimensions were set for the wheel-base of all carriages and carts. In an attempt to end all opposition, over 400 scholars were buried alive, and all books were burnt, except for those on technology, divination, medicine and agriculture. Land reclamation（开垦荒地）, tilling of the soil（深耕） and weaving of textiles were encouraged. As a defense against the northern nomads（游牧民族）, hundreds and thousands of peasants were conscripted to join up and extend the walls of the former northern states into the Great Wall of China. The completed Great Wall stretched some ten thousand li (里, around 5,000 kilometers).

Though Qin Shihuang's contribution to China's civilization is great, yet in traditional culture he is remembered mainly for his tyranny and cruelty. Not long after Qin Shihuang's death, a rebellion broke out—the first peasant uprising in China's history, led by Chen Sheng (陈胜) and Wu Guang (吴广), and the Qin Empire was overthrown.

The Han Dynasty （汉朝, 206 B.C.E.—220 A.D.）

Drawing lessons of defeat from the Qin Dynasty, the early Han ruling class adopted a policy of rehabilitation (休养生息). As a result, the Han Dynasty saw peace and prosperity. Agriculture and handicraft made rapid development, commerce flourished and there were a variety of notable achievements in culture and science, including Sima Qian's *The Records of the Historians* (司马迁:《史记》) and the invention of the seismograph (地动仪) by Zhang Heng (张衡). The invention of paper, perhaps China's greatest contribution to the world culture, was also a

The seismograph invented by Zhang Heng

product of this period. The Confucian classics were recovered, re-edited and commented on, and Confucianism became the most important philosophy, thus the supremacy of the Confucian school was established. Han Wudi (汉武帝) also sent Zhang Qian (张骞) on friendly expeditions to the Western Regions, reaching Rome, opening up the Silk Road (丝绸之路) to the West.

Wei （魏, 220 A.D.—265 A.D.）
Jin （晋, 265 A.D.—420 A.D.）
Southern and Northern Dynasties （南北朝, 420 A.D.—581 A.D.）

With the downfall of the Han Dynasty, China entered the Three Kingdoms Period, in which Chinese territory was divided between the states of Wei (魏), Shu Han (蜀汉) and Wu (吴). Burning and pillaging ravaged the country in the last years of the Han Dynasty, and the Three Kingdoms arose as contenders for imperial power. The famous novel *Romance of the Three Kingdoms* (《三国演义》) by Luo Guanzhong (罗贯中) was based on the historical facts of this period. At the end of this period, China was briefly united during the Jin Dynasty (晋朝, 265 A.D.—420 A.D.) but this was followed by a period of division during the Southern and Northern Dynasties (420 A.D.—589 A.D.).

In the period from the Three Kingdoms to the Southern and Northern Dynasties, there appeared some great literary and scientific figures, among whom were Zu Chongzi (祖冲之), who made notable contributions to mathematics, astronomy and engineering, especially the calculation of the relation of the circle's circumference to its diameter; Wang Xizhi (王羲之), one of the greatest Chinese calligraphers; and Gu Kaizhi (顾恺之), who was among the most famous painters in China.

The Sui Dynasty （隋朝, 581 A.D.—618 A.D.）

Zhaozhou Bridge

After a coup d'etat ([kuːdeɪ'taː] 军事政变) in the northern capital of Luoyang, Sui Wendi (隋文帝) proclaimed himself emperor in the north. In 589 A.D., he reunited the empire. Taxation and conscription were reduced, and new public works began. The most outstanding achievements were the construction of the Grand Canal (大运河) and Zhaozhou Bridge (赵州桥). The former, linking the Yellow and Yangtze Rivers from Beijing to Hangzhou, was a project of economic and political significance. The latter remains the world's oldest stone arch bridge. But the Sui Dynasty also squandered huge resources of money and man-power on the building of the grand palaces and pleasure gardens in Luoyang, and on wars against the neighboring states. Following the collapse of his frontier policy, and a series of disastrous wars against Koguryo (高句丽), the Sui Yangdi (隋炀帝) was assassinated in 618 A.D. One of the rebel officers, Li Yuan (李渊) seized power, and began the Tang Dynasty.

Also in the Sui Dynasty, a nationwide examination system, called civil service examination (科举考试), was instituted to select officials of various levels of the government.

The Tang Dynasty （唐朝, 618 A.D.—907 A.D.）

The Tang Dynasty was a prime time in ancient Chinese history, known for its prosperity of economy, flourishing of culture, high development of agriculture, commerce and handicrafts, and close relations with the neighboring regions. The route to the Western regions was reopened, and trade accelerated. Tang's architecture was famous for the grandeur and magnificence of its palaces, temples and pagodas.

The Tang period was the renaissance of classical literature. Nearly 50,000 poems written in this period are still in existence. They are beyond comparison in richness of contents and a variety of forms and styles. Among the thousands of poets of the Tang Dynasty the best known are Li Bai（李白）, Du Fu（杜甫）and Bai Juyi（白居易）.

It was in this period that Xuan Zang（玄奘）, a Buddhist monk and scholar, was sent to Western regions. In 627 A.D. , he set out from Chang'an（长安 , currently Xi'an）of China to India. He went through Central Asia, and after untold hardships, finally reached India, where he lived for 15 years visiting many famous temples. He studied Buddhist classics and learned the Buddhist doctrines from the Indian monk scholars. After returning to Chang'an, he translated 75 Buddhist scriptures（1,335 volumes）into Chinese. He also wrote an account of his trip, entitled *Records of the Western Travels*（《大唐西域记》）, an important reference for researchers to study the history and geography of ancient India, Nepal and Pakistan, as well as Central Asia. The novel *Journey to the West*（《西游记》）, is a mythological account of his trip to India. The main part of the novel is a series of episodes relating to the adventures of Tang Seng（唐僧） on a pilgrimage to the Western Region（i.e. India）. He is accompanied by several mythological figures, such as Sun Wukong（孙悟空 , the Monkey King）, the real hero of the novel, who has strong magic power and always outwits various kinds of ghosts and monsters.

Another Buddhist monk, sent to Japan in the Tang period, was Jian Zhen（鉴真）. He tried five times to sail from Yangzhou（扬州） in Jiangsu Province to Japan. Each time he failed and he eventually became blind. On his sixth try, accompanied by 24 disciples, he reached southern Kyushu. That was in 754 A.D., and he was then 67. The next year, in Nara, Japan's capital at that time, he began to preach Buddhist teachings and became the founder of the Ritsugku Sect in Japan. Accompanying him to Japan were architects, artists, doctors and pharmacists. They took many books with them, and did much to stimulate the cultural exchange between the two countries. The magnificent Tang-styled Toshodai Temple（唐昭提寺） at Nara still looks much the same as it did when it was built under Jian Zhen's directions. Jian Zhen lived for nearly 10 years in Japan and died there in 763 A.D.

The Five Dynasties （五代, 907 A.D.—960 A.D.）
The Song Dynasty （宋朝, 960 A.D.—1279 A.D.）
The Liao Dynasty （辽朝, 907 A.D.—1125 A.D.）
The Jin Dynasty （金朝, 1115 A.D.—1234 A.D.）

After the fall of the Tang Dynasty, and for the next 53 years, power fell into the hands of warlords and this period is known in Chinese history as "the period of Five Dynasties and Ten Kingdoms" （五代十国）. Eventually, in the year 960, one of the warlords, Zhao Kuangyin（赵匡胤） succeeded in reuniting the greater part of the country and founded the Song Dynasty. He himself is called in history Song Taizu（宋太祖）. However, the northeast remained under the control of a group of Tartar nomads, known as the Khitan （契丹）, who had taken the name of the Liao Dynasty. Concurrently the northwest was occupied by another group of Tartars known as the Xixia（西夏）.

The Song emperors made several attempts to recover these regions but failed. This was the result not only of military weakness, but of general internal weakness. Then the Song emperors united with the Jin Tartars to attack the Khitan in order to restore the northeast provinces to the Song. But the Jin Tartars not only overcame the Khitan, but moved on to conquer the whole of the north of the Huai River（淮河） and in 1125 founded the Jin Dynasty. In 1127, the Song capital of Kaifeng fell, and the emperor and his heir were taken into captivity. That was the end of the Northern Song Dynasty. The remnants of the Song followers moved to the south and made Hangzhou（杭州） its capital. This was known in history as the Southern Song Dynasty, controlling only the Yangtze River valley and the regions of the south.

One interesting phenomenon that should be noted is that from the tenth century onwards, the constant pressure on north China by the nomads had led to more and more of the wealthy families fleeing to the south. So when the Northern Song fell, the south was already economically developed. Though losing half of the country to the northern nomads, the Southern Song rulers and gentry still lived a life of extravagance and ease. Among the daughters of wealthy families, the custom of foot binding was popular. They believed that small feet would make them look graceful and sexual. If they were captured by the northern Tartars, they were not taken away because they could not walk long distances. Though less harmful than the 19th century European custom of waist-binding, it served the same purpose of emphasizing the upper-class woman's dependence on man as his plaything. Peasant women who had to work in the fields with their men folk were not subjected to this cruel fashion.

Though the Song period was one of extreme military and political weakness, its science and technology, literature and art were developing rapidly. There were various reasons. One of them was the opening of foreign trade. Huge maritime centers grew up as ports such as Canton and Hangzhou, and from them great ocean-going junks carrying Chinese silk and porcelains sailed to India, the Middle East and East Africa. The issue of paper money also accelerated trade and commerce. Merchants had developed a system of depositing stocks or coins in a certain area in exchange for notes which could be cashed in another area. The invention of printing by movable type by Bi Sheng（毕昇） stimulated literary creation. The compass, which had been invented by the Chinese at a much earlier date, was used in navigation during this period.

The misfortunes of the country made many men of letters take up their pens to express their sorrows over the country and their frustration in life. Influenced by exotic music, they created a new form of poetry consisting of lines of different lengths—*Ci*（词）. The most famous *Ci* poets were Liu Yong（柳永）, Zhou Bangyan（周邦彦）, Su Shi（苏轼） and Xin Qiji（辛弃疾）. Song landscape painting and Song porcelain are renowned throughout the world even today. And the craftsmanship, the elegance and simplicity of Song ceramics have never been surpassed.

It was not only in the arts that Song excelled. In science and technology, the period was also famous for the development of the magnetic compass, gunpowder and printing. The first text in the world to describe a magnetic compass clearly（then called "south-pointing needle"）was the work entitled *Dreams Pool Essays*（《梦溪笔谈》）, published by the Song mathematician Shen Kuo（沈括）.

The Yuan Dynasty （元朝, **1206 A.D.—1368 A.D.**）
The Ming Dynasty （明朝, **1368 A.D.—1644 A.D.**）
The Qing Dynasty （清朝, **1616 A.D.—1911 A.D.**）

In 1276, the Mongols captured the Southern Song capital of Hangzhou, and later the whole of China passed under the Mongol yoke. Kublai Khan（忽必烈汗） was proclaimed Emperor of all China and moved the capital to Beijing. That was the beginning of the Yuan Dynasty.

But the Mongol Empire lasted less than a hundred years, for they distrusted the Han people and appointed non-Hans to the top administrative posts. This weakened the Yuan rule, and during the 1360s, a peasant revolt led by Zhu Yuanzhang（朱元璋） captured Nanjing and gained control of the Yantze River valley. The Mongols were driven northwards and in 1368 Zhu was proclaimed Emperor, thus ushering in the three centuries of the Ming Dynasty. The Ming Dynasty was followed by the Qing Dynasty, during which the feudal period in China gradually drew to a close. Under the Qing rule, China gradually declined and was invaded by European powers.

Zaju（杂剧）, or drama, was the greatest achievement in the literature of the Yuan Dynasty. Three hundred and forty-five *Zaju* plays have been handed down, 63 of which were written by the well-known playwright Guan Hanqin（关汉卿）. His *Snow in Midsummer*（《窦娥冤》） and Wang Shifu's *The Western Chamber*（王实甫:《西厢记》） are masterpieces which have been widely read over the centuries. The Ming and Qing Dynasties were great periods of fiction and drama. It was in this period, the four great full-length novels appeared: *Outlaws of the Marsh* by Shi Naian（施耐庵:《水浒传》）, *Romance of the Three Kingdoms* by Luo Guanzhong（罗贯中:《三国演义》）, *Journey to the West* by Wu Chengen（吴承恩:《西游记》） and *A Dream of Red Mansions* by Cao Xueqin（曹雪芹:《红楼梦》）.

As a reaction against the Mongol rule, the Ming Dynasty sought to restore Chinese tradition and learning. A great deal of energy was devoted to compilation work. The chief writings inherited from the past, including many rare and unique works were copied into over 22,937 volumes of a vast encyclopedia called *Yongle Dadian*（《永乐大典》）. Unfortunately, the greatest part of this collection was lost during the disorders of the nineteenth century.

The early years of the Ming Dynasty also saw the development of a navy: Chinese sea power, under the admiral Zheng He（郑和）, reached Borneo（婆罗洲——加里曼丹旧称）, Java（爪哇）, Sumatra（苏门答腊）, Ceylon（锡兰）, India and East Africa.

Modern Period （1840 A.D.—Present）

The Opium War was the turning point in Chinese history which marked the close of the ancient Chinese period and the beginning of modern history. From 1840 on imperialists made continuous inroads into China, and China gradually became a state of semi-feudal, semi-colonial status. The Chinese people suffered a lot in the succeeding century but their resistance grew more determined and powerful. From the middle of the 19th century, the Chinese people launched numerous revolutionary movements against the rule of feudalism and imperialism, such as the Taiping Revolution（太平天国起义）, the Yihetuan Movement（义和团运动） and the Revolution of 1911（辛亥革命）.

Starting from Jintian（金田） village in Guangxi Province, the Taiping forces made rapid military progress. One of their favorite tactics in attacking cities was to use their contingent of coal miners to dig tunnels to undermine the defending walls. The incompetence of the government forces was also a help. As the Taiping armies advanced, they picked up strength. They took Nanjing in 1853 and founded the "Heavenly Kingdom of Great Peace"（太平天国）. The failure of the Taiping uprising was due to the internal conflict of the leading group and the inadequate implementation of the stated policies. For example,

Hong Xiuquan（洪秀全）and other leaders kept numerous concubines despite the Taiping call for monogamy（一夫一妻制）.

The Qing Dynasty, the last of China's feudal dynasties, was finally overthrown by the Revolution of 1911 led by Sun Yat-sen（孙中山）. One year later, the Republic of China（中华民国） was founded under his leadership.

With the introduction of Marxism and Leninism into China and under the influence of the October Revolution in Russia, the May 4th Movement broke out in 1919 and in 1921 the Chinese Communist Party was founded, thus beginning a new period in Chinese history. Under the leadership of the Chinese Communist Party, the Chinese people fought three civil wars and Anti-Japanese War, and after bitter and resolute struggles, finally overthrew the rule of imperialism, feudalism and bureaucratic capitalism, and established the People's Republic of China in 1949.

· *Seminar* ·

Tell one or two of the historical stories described in the book or out of the book.

Chapter Two

Philosophy and Classics

- Confucius and Confucianism
- Lao Zi and Taoism
- Buddhism
- Mo Zi and Moism
- Han Fei Zi and Legalism
- *Four Books and Five Classics*

The rich and, in many ways, unique civilization of China owes much in its shaping to the widespread influence of Confucianism, Taoism and Buddhism, which are generally regarded as the three roots of Chinese culture. The influence of these three philosophies, especially of Confucianism, not only came to predominate in China for more than two thousand years but also was powerful in shaping the social and political life of some neiboring countries. In this chapter we will discuss them one by one with our commentaries.

I
Confucius and Confucianism

Confucius

Confucius (Kong Zi) is regarded as the "Great and Revered Teacher" (至圣先师), a teacher for all generations (万世师表). He has laid down the foundation of Chinese education. From the dawn of civilization to the Revolution of 1911 (辛亥革命), he has so deeply influenced the life and thought of the Chinese people that he is regarded as the moulder of the Chinese mind and character. His thoughts and teachings are regarded as the symbol of traditional Chinese culture.

Confucius (551 B.C.E.—479 B.C.E.), styled Zhongni (字仲尼), born in today's Qufu (曲阜), Shandong Province, was the great thinker, statesman and educator in the late Spring and Autumn Period and the founder of Confucianism. Poor as he was when young, he was bright and diligent. As a result, he became a learned and versatile man. He was the first in China to establish "private schools" and was said to have taught 3,000 students, among whom 72 were talents.

Confucius inherited and developed upon the teachings of his predecessors and, catering to situations of his time, established his own school of thought. Ideologically, Confucius was a firm believer in "the ordinance of Heaven" (天命论), holding that "Death and life have their determined appointment; riches and honors depend upon Heaven" (生死有命，富贵在天). He preaches *Ren* (仁, benevolence) and *Yi* (义, righteousness), requiring the people to "subdue one's self and return to propriety" (克己复礼). Defining the term *Ren* as "love for all men", Confucius advocates "reciprocity" (恕) — "Do not do to others what you do not want others to do to you (己所不欲，勿施于人)." Confucius attaches such great importance to *Ren* as to regard it as a universal solution to all human problems. For a definite period of time and to some extent, the Confucian theory of *Ren* complied with the interests of the common people and appealed to the middle and lower rank scholars and officials. With the improvement by the Neo-Confucians Mencius and Xun Zi, Confucianism achieved prevailing influence among the feudal rulers. By the Western Han Dynasty, Emperor Wu（汉武帝）adopted the proposal of the well-known scholar Dong Zhongshu（董仲舒）to "revere Confucianism and reject all other schools of thought"（罢黜百家，独尊儒术）. Ever since, Confucianism had dominated the ancient Chinese politics, ideology and life.

About Kong Zi's Family Line

Kong Zi's forefathers belonged to the Shang royals. After the downfall of the Shang Dynasty, King Wu of Zhou（周武王）conferred the royal title upon Wei Ziqi（微子启）, a loyal and righteous minister of Shang to hold office in the State of Song（宋）. Wei Ziqi was succeeded by his younger brother Wei Zhong（微仲）who was Kong Zi's ancestor.

Many generations passed. Jia（嘉）, the sixth generation of Kong's line of ancestors, adopted "Kong"（孔）as the family name. Thus, from then on, all his descendants were surnamed "Kong". In order to avoid the upheaval in the State of Song, Kong Zi's grandfather Kong Fengsu（孔防叔）moved to the state of Lu（鲁）.

Kong Zi's father Su Lianghe（叔梁纥）was one of the three famous warriors in Lu. He married Shi Yaoying（施曜英）and had nine daughters, and his concubine gave birth to a son named Meng Pi（孟皮）, who was lame. According to the ancient customs, daughters and handicapped sons could not be made heirs. So Su Lianghe had to have the second marriage in order to have an heir. He went to propose to the family of Yan Xiang（颜襄）, a well-known intellectual in the area. Yan summoned his three daughters and said, "Su Lianghe is a man of virtue. Any of you would like to accept his offer of marriage?" The elder and second daughters kept silent. But the youngest daughter Yan Zheng（颜征）answered, "I would like to accept the offer in compliance with father's wishes." So the sixteen-year-old Yan Zheng married the sixty-four-year-old Su Lianghe. Because of the great gap of age between husband and wife, Su Lianghe could not take his young wife home and Yan Zheng had to live in an ancestral temple on the hillside of Ni Shan（尼山）. This is , as Sima Qian（司马迁）put it, an "outdoor union."

Su Lianghe and Yan Zheng spent their marriage life happily. They lived in harmony, loving and caring for each other. Legend has it that one night, Yan Zheng had a dream, seeing a colorful cloud drifting from the northwest and descending in front of their house. The cloud dispersed, and a unicorn appeared, smiling at her. Before long, Yan Zheng was pregnant. Eleven months later, Yan Zheng had another dream. In her dream, she saw two dragons coming down from Heaven, keeping watching over Ni Shan. Two genial fairies with joss sticks appeared from the clouds, waving towards her. At dawn next morning, she woke up to find that rosy clouds were spreading over the sky. She was delighted and joyful. As usual, she took a walk along the hill-side. After a hundred steps of walk, she felt the move of the baby inside her. The baby raised the first cry of life before she could return home.

Su Lianghe hurried to her and Yan Zheng told her husband what had happened, saying, "Thank Heaven! We are bestowed a son. Please give him a name." After thinking for a while, Su Lianghe said, "Our child is born on the hill-side of Ni Shan. Just look at his head, the middle part is like a basin surrounded by hills. He must have got the spirit of Ni Shan. Let's name him Qiu（丘，'hill'）. Since he is the second son of the family, let him be styled Zhong Ni（仲尼）（Zhong, 仲, second; Ni, 尼, Ni Shan）."

The Ethical Principles of Confucianism

Confucianism had been regarded as an ethic-political system in ancient China. For more than two thousand years it has moulded and shaped the civilization of China and exerted a profound influence upon almost one-fourth of the human race.

Confucianism has left us a rich literary heritage known as the *Four Books and Five Classics: The Great Learning*（《大学》）, *The Doctrine of Mean*（《中庸》）, *Analects*（《论语》）, and *Mencius*（《孟子》）; *Book of Change*（《易经》）, *Book of History*（《尚书》）, *Book of Odes*（《诗经》）, *Book of Rites*（《礼记》）and *Spring and Autumn Annals*（《春秋》）. For six centuries（1313 A.D.—1905 A.D.）, these texts became the elementary requirements of Chinese education in the feudal society and served as the basis of the civil service examination（科举考试）by which scholars were selected for official posts at various levels of the government.

The ethical principle of Confucianism is its discovery of the ultimate in the moral character of human relationships in which Confucius offered the solution for the ills and evils of his day. That is the well-known Five Relationships: ruler—minister, father—son, husband—wife, elder—younger brother, and friend—friend. The responsibilities ensuing from these relationships are mutual and reciprocal. A minister owes loyalty to his ruler, and a child filial respect to his parent. But the ruler must care for his subjects（臣民）, and the parent for the child. Just as Confucius said of the doctrine of reciprocity and neighborliness: "Within the four seas all men are brothers（四海之内皆兄弟）." "Do not do to others what you would not want others to do to you（己所不欲，勿施于人）."

Confucius's central doctrine is that of the virtue of *Ren* (仁). What is *Ren*? *Ren* is translated variously as goodness, benevolence, humanity, and human-heartedness. In short, *Ren* means affection and love. "A man of *Ren* loves others." Fan Chi asked about "*Ren*", Confucius said, "Love all men." (樊迟问仁, 子曰: "爱人。")

The ethical thought of Confucius can be summed up as the following five cardinal virtues:

1. *Ren* (仁): the will to show benevolence to others (the root).

2. *Yi* (义): righteousness by justice (the trunk).

3. *Li* (礼): moral ways of conduct (the branches).

4. *Zhi* (智): wisdom (the flower).

5. *Xin* (信): faithfulness (the fruit).

Confucianism's greatest contribution to the Chinese nation is its shaping and moulding of the Chinese character and national soul and its founding of the complete system of knowledge. Just as Dr. Sun Yat-sen said: "Therefore the old morals of loyalty and piety (忠孝), affection and love (仁爱), faithfulness and righteousness (信义), are superior to those of the foreign countries, let alone that of peace and harmony (和平). These high standards of morals are our national spirit."

The complete system of knowledge is laid down in the book of *the Great Learning*:

> The way of the Great Learning lies in illustrating virtue, rejuvenating the people, and reaching perfection.... The ancients who wished to illustrate virtue throughout the world would first govern well their own state. To govern their state well, they would first regulate their families. To regulate their families, they would first cultivate their own personality. To cultivate their personality they would rectify their minds. To rectify their minds, they would first strive to be sincere in their thoughts. Wishing for sincerity in their thoughts, they would expand their knowledge. The expansion of knowledge lay in the investigation of things.

【原文】

大学之道, 在明明德, 在亲民, 在止于至善。……古之君子欲明明德于天下者, 先治其国。欲治其国者, 先齐其家。欲齐其家者, 先修其身。欲修其身者, 先正其心。欲正其心者, 先诚其意。欲诚其意者, 先致其知。致知在格物。[《大学》·孔经]

【今译】

最大的学问, 在于弘扬道德, 使人们鼎新革故, 从而达到至善至美的理想境界。……古之君子要想发扬光大美德于天下, 先要治理好自己的国家; 要想治理好自己的国家, 先要整治好自己的家庭; 要想整治好自己的家庭, 先要修养好自己的本身; 要想修养好自己的本身, 先端正自己的思想; 要想端正自己的思想, 先要使自己的意念诚实；要想使自己的意念诚实，先要获得知识。获得知识的目的，在于懂得事物的道理。

How Confucius Moulded the Soul of Our Nation and Shaped the National Character?

What is our national spirit and national character? It can be summed up in eight words: loyalty and reciprocity（忠恕），affection and love（仁爱），faithfulness and righteousness（信义），peace and harmony（和平）. Now let's see how Confucius laid down these principles which have shaped our national character for two thousand years.

Loyalty and Reciprocity（忠恕）

Confucius said, "Shen! My teaching contains one principle that runs through it all." "Yes," replied Zeng Zi. When Confucius had left the room, the disciples asked: "What did he mean?" Zeng Zi replied: "Our master's teaching is simply this: loyalty and reciprocity."

子曰："参乎，吾道一以贯之。"曾子曰："唯。"子出，门人问曰："何谓也？"曾子曰："夫子之道，忠恕而已矣。"

《论语》四篇十五节

（今译：孔子说："参呀，我讲的道理是由一个基本思想贯穿始终的。"曾子答："是的"。孔子出去以后，同学们问曾子："这是什么意思？"曾子说："先生的道，就是忠恕罢了。"）

Zi Gong asked: "Is there any one word that can serve as a principle for the conduct of life?" Confucius said, "Perhaps the word 'reciprocity': Do not do to others what you would not want others to do to you."

子贡问曰："有一言而可以终身行之者乎？"子曰："其恕乎！己所不欲，勿施于人。"

《论语》十五篇廿四节

（今译：子贡问道："有没有一个字是可以终身奉行的呢？"孔子说："那就是恕字吧，自己不愿意要的，不要强加给别人。"）

· *Comments* ·

Loyalty—loyal to the country, loyal to the people, loyal to one's own conscience, loyal to your friend, husband or wife, isn't it a high standard of morals?

Reciprocity—to think in the position of others, to come to the rescue when others are in difficulty, treat other people as you would do to yourself（推己及人），be considerate of others. Isn't it a good tradition that we should follow?

Affection and Love（仁爱）

Fan Chi asked what "*Ren*（仁）" is. Confucius said, "Love others."

樊迟问仁，子曰爱人。

《论语》十二篇二十四节

（今译：樊迟问："什么是仁？"孔子说："爱所有的人。"）

Confucius said, "The humane man, desiring to establish himself, seeks to establish others; desiring himself to succeed, helps others to succeed. To judge others by what one knows of oneself is the method of achieving '*Ren*'."

子曰："夫仁者，己欲立而立人，己欲达而达人。能近取譬，可谓仁之方也已。"

《论语》六篇卅节

（今译：至于仁，就是自己想自立，也就帮助别人自立；自己想要通达，也帮助别人通达。能就近以自己的心作比较而推及别人，可以说就是为仁的方法了。）

Men of virtue will not seek to live at the expense of their virtue. On the contrary they will sacrifice their lives to preserve their virtue.

志士仁人，无求生以害仁，有杀身以成仁。

《论语》十五篇九节

（今译：志士仁人，没有贪生怕死而损害仁德的，只有牺牲性命成全仁德。）

· *Comments* ·

These maxims have become the motto（座右铭）of many Chinese revolutionaries who, at the critical moment of life and death, would rather die than surrender themselves to the enemy, just to preserve their principles and to keep their integrity of morals.

Faithfulness and Righteousness（信义）

Confucius said, "Riches and honor acquired by unrighteous means are to me as drifting clouds."

子曰："不义而富且贵，于我如浮云。"

《论语》七篇十六节

（今译：干不正当的事情而得来的富贵，对于我犹如转瞬即逝的浮云一般。）

Zi Gong asked what a gentleman is, Confucius said, "A gentleman first practises what he preaches and then preaches what he practises.

子贡问君子。子曰："先行其言而后从之。"

《论语》二篇十三节

（今译：子贡问怎样做一个君子。孔子说："先践行你要说的话，然后再说。"）

In the face of benefits, one would think of righteousness; in the face of danger, one is prepared to give up his life; in long-term poverty, one does not forget his principle—such a man may be regarded as a perfect man.

见利思义，见危授命，久要不忘平生之言，亦可以为成人矣。

《论语》十四篇十五节

（今译：见到利益能想到符不符合原则；遇到危险愿意付出生命；长久处于贫困仍不忘记自己的诺言，也就可以说是完人了。）

· *Comments*·

These words of Confucius have been esteemed by the Chinese people as a high standard of morals and spiritual strength. Later Mencius developed these words into "One, who would not corrupt before riches and honors, nor swerve in poverty nor bend under pressure and power, can be considered as a great man" (富贵不能淫, 贫贱不能移, 威武不能屈, 此之谓大丈夫。——《孟子·滕文公（下）》)

Peace and Harmony（和平）

Isn't he a man of virtue, who doesn't feel annoyed when others do not understand him?
子曰："人不知而不愠，不亦君子乎？"

《论语》一篇一节

（今译：别人不了解自己而不恼怒，不就是个品德高尚的君子吗？）

A Man of virtue has nothing to contend with others for.
君子无所争。

《论语》三篇七节

（今译：君子没有什么可以与人相争的事情。）

A knowledgeable man looks as if he were void of knowledge; a talented man is broadminded, not annoyed even if he is offended.
有若无，实若虚，犯而不校。

《论语》八篇五节

（今译：有学问却空若无物，有才华却虚怀若谷，受人冒犯也不计较。）

A man of virtue is always at ease without pride. An inferior man is proud without ease.
君子泰而不骄，小人骄而不泰。

《论语》十三篇廿六节

（今译：君子安详舒展而不骄傲，小人骄傲而不安详舒展。）

· *Comments*·

It is a very high standard of virtue to keep balance in mind, to be calm and at ease when you are in difficulty or trouble, misunderstood or even offended by others. If everybody cultivates himself in this way, the country and the whole world will become peaceful and harmonious.

Selected Readings from *Analects*

Confucius said, "Isn't it a pleasure to learn and then review what you've learned from time to time? Isn't it a joy to meet friends from afar? Isn't he a man of virtue, who doesn't feel annoyed when others do not understand him?"

【原文】

子曰："学而时习之，不亦说乎？有朋自远方来，不亦乐乎？人不知而不愠，不亦君子乎？"

【今译】

孔子说："学习然后经常地练习，不是件很愉快的事吗？有志同道合的朋友从远方来，不是件很快乐的事吗？不因为别人不了解自己而恼怒，不就是个品德高尚的君子吗？"

Confucius said, "At fifteen, I set my heart on learning; at thirty, I was firmly established; at forty, I had no more puzzles; at fifty, I could understand Heaven's will; at sixty, my ears were attuned; at seventy, I could follow my heart's desires without transgressing what was right."

【原文】

子曰："吾十有五而志于学，三十而立，四十而不惑，五十而知天命，六十而耳顺，七十而从心所欲不逾矩。"

【今译】

孔子说："我十五岁就立志学习，三十岁能自立，四十岁遇事而不迷惑，五十岁知天命，六十岁能正确对待各种意见，七十岁能随心所欲而不越出规矩。"

Confucius said, "Learning without thinking is labor lost; thinking without learning is perilous."

【原文】

子曰："学而不思则罔，思而不学则殆。"

【今译】

孔子说："只学习而不思考，就会迷惑受骗；只思考而不学习，那是危险的事情。"

Duke She asked Zi Lu about Confucius, but Zi Lu gave no answer. Later, Confucius said, "Why didn't you tell him that I am a man who neglects his meals in his eager pursuit of knowledge, who forgets his sorrows in his enjoyment of books, and is unaware of old age coming on?"

【原文】

叶公问孔子于子路，子路不对。子曰："女奚不曰，其为人也，发愤忘食，乐以忘忧，不知老之将至云尔。"

【今译】

叶公问子路孔子是个怎样的人，子路不答。孔子说："你为什么不说，他这个人呀，发愤读书，连饭也忘记吃了；乐在书中，把一切忧愁都忘记了，连自己快要老了都不知道。他不过如此而已。"

Confucius said, "When traveling in company of two other people, I could find my teachers. I would learn from their good points and guard against their bad ones."

【原文】

子曰："三人行，必有我师焉。择其善者而从之，其不善者而改之。"

【今译】

孔子说："三人同行，其中一定有可为我师的人。我可以学习他们的优点和长处。对于他们的缺点和短处，如果我有的话则改正。"

Confucius said, "A man of virtue is open-minded and always at ease; a man of meanness is full of distress at all times."

【原文】

子曰："君子坦荡荡，小人长戚戚。"

【今译】

孔子说："君子心胸开阔，神态安详；小人却经常愁眉不展。"

Confucius said, "You may be able to carry off the commander from a whole army, but you cannot take away the will of a common folk."

【原文】

子曰:"三军可夺帅也,匹夫不可夺志也。"

【今译】

孔子说:"你或许能从三军中夺帅,却难夺去一个普通百姓的意志。"

When Confucius was traveling to Wei, Ran You drove the carriage for him. Confucius observed: "What a big population!" Ran You said, "People are so numerous, what should we do for them?" "Enrich them, " was the Master's reply. "And when they are rich, what next should be done?" Confucius said, "Educate them."

【原文】

子适卫,冉有仆。子曰:"庶矣哉。"冉有曰:"既庶矣,又何加焉? " 曰:"富之。"曰:"既富矣,又何加焉? "曰:"教之。"

【今译】

孔子去到卫国,冉有为他赶车。孔子说:"人真多呀!"冉有说:"人口这么多,下一步该做什么呢? "孔子曰:"使他们富起来。"冉有说:"富起来了又怎么办? "孔子说:"教育他们。"

Confucius said, "There is no distinction of classes in education."

【原文】

子曰:"有教无类。"

【今译】

孔子说:"人人都有接受教育的权利,不应该加以分类区别。"

Mencius and His Philosophy

Mencius (372 B.C.E.—289 B.C.E.) is regarded as the second sage in the Confucian school. Only two Chinese philosophers have the honor of being known to the Western world by a Latinized name. The first is Confucius and the second Mencius, whose name is Mong Zi (孟子). Mencius inherited and developed Confucianism and carried it to a new height. His philosophy, together with Confucius's, is known as "the philosophies of Kong Zi and Meng Zi (孔孟之道)" in the history of Chinese culture.

The book, *Mencius*, bearing the master's name, has recorded the thoughts, sayings and deeds of this second most important Confucians. Compared to *Analects*, which is composed of brief, laconic and provocative sentences, lacking context and difficult to interpret, the articles in *Mencius* are of greater length, logical, argumentative and persuasive, covering a variety of subjects, greatly influencing the writing of essays in the dynasties that followed. Many ideas in *Analects* are not explained clearly, leaving a great

Mencius

deal of room for different interpretations. The ideas in *Mencius* are more articulate.

Mencius inherited Confucius's theory of *Ren*（仁）, but he added to it a second concept—*Yi*（义）, meaning "righteousness", "propriety" or "dutifulness." He was even more insistent than Confucius on the moral qualities of humanity and the sense of duty that makes a true ruler. He advocated that in the constitution of a state, "the people rank the highest, the land and grain comes next, and the ruler counts the least（民为贵，社稷次之，君为轻）." It is very commendable of him to put forth such advanced thought in a time when the emperor was in the supreme position and all power was in his hands. According to Mencius, a governor exists for the sake of the governed, to give people peace and wealth and lead them by education and examples of virtue. If a ruler neglects his responsibility, or even misuses his power and oppresses the people, the people have the right to discontinue their loyalty to him or even rise against him.

It is this promotion of the common people and their right to revolution that made some rulers regards *Mencius* as a dangerous book. Like Confucius, Mencius also failed to find a ruler who would listen to him and put his theories into practice. So he spent most of his time teaching disciples.

Mencius was a tender-minded philosopher. He believed that all men are born virtuous. Every person can be a sage（人皆可以为尧舜）. They have the inclination towards goodness, just as natural as the inclination of water to flow downward. All the social corruptions and perversions are due to the distortion of human nature and the falling away of man's character from its original goodness. It is the neglect and abuse of innate goodness that leads men into evil doings. Once the individual has recovered his original goodness and the state returned to the purity and order of ancient times, all the evils in the individual and in society will vanish. This is the core of Mencius's doctrine, the orthodoxy of the Confucian school.

A famous dispute about human nature arose between Gao Zi（告子）and Mencius when Gao Zi said, "Appetites for food and sex are human nature（食色，性也）." Mencius did not contradict with this statement; he even admitted that desires and appetites constitute the greatest part of human nature. Therefore "slight is the difference between man and the beast. The common man loses this difference, while the gentleman retains it."（人之所以异于禽兽者几希，庶民去之，君子存之。）It is this slight difference that sets man apart from animals.

There are lots of legends about Mencius which are popular among the Chinese people. Let's quote some of them for you to enjoy.

Mother Mong Cut Apart the Cloth to Teach the Son a Lesson（孟母断布教子）

When Mencius was a boy, he was reciting his lessons one day while his mother was weaving. Suddenly he stopped and then went on again. His mother knew that he could not remember the text. She called him to her and asked, "Why did you stop?" The boy answered, "I lost the thread, but I picked it up again." His mother took out a pair of scissors and cut what she had woven, saying "what you are doing is just like cutting apart the cloth." From then on, Mencius never repeated the same mistake.

Mother Mong Removed the Living Place Three Times to Provide the Son with a Good Environment（孟母三易其居教子）

When Mencius was a boy, their house was near a graveyard. The boys played a game of grave-digging and Mencius was most energetic at the game—building the tombs and burying the dead. "This is no place for my child." said Mother Mong, so she moved to live next to a market. This time Mencius played with the boys to peddle the "goods." Mother Mong said once more, "This is no place for my child." Once again she moved to live near a school. This time Mencius played at reading and practised rituals. "This is truly a place for my child, " said the mother and she settled down. Mencius learned the six arts and became a learned scholar. Mother Mong was a great mother who knew the significance of gradual transformation（潜移默化）.

Mother Mong Regulated the Family（孟母齐家）

After Mencius got married, one day when he was about to enter his private chamber, he found his wife scantily clad. Mencius was displeased and left without entering. His wife went to Mother Mong and said, "I have heard that ceremony between husband and wife does not extend to the private chamber. Just now I was relaxing in my room and my husband, seeing me, showed anger in his face. This is treating me as a visitor. I beg to be allowed to return to my parents." After hearing that, Mother Mong summoned Mencius and told him, "According to the *Book of Rites*, on entering the gate of a house, ask which members of the family are in, so as to pay one's respects. On ascending the hall, raise your voice, so as to give notice. On entering the room, lower your eyes. This is for fear of seeing others at fault. Now you expect others to conform to the *Book of Rites* while failing yourself to see the import. Is this wide of mark?"

Mencius apologized and kept his wife. From this story we know how Mother Mong taught her son to be a man of virtue.

· *Seminar* ·

1. What kind of man is Confucius?

2. Comment on the book *Analects*.

3. What is the national spirit and national character of the Chinese nation?

II
Lao Zi and Taoism

Lao Zi

Lao Zi is regarded as the father of Chinese philosophy. With keen eyes and great wisdom, he observed the laws of heaven and earth, the changes of nature, as well as failure and success, existence and extinction, bad and good fortune in human society. In the history of Chinese philosophy, no one can be compared with Lao Zi who so extensively and thoroughly studied the laws of motion in the world. Many of Lao Zi's dialectical aphorisms have been handed down from generation to generation, becoming the spiritual wealth of the Chinese culture. Many of his viewpoints and principles of life such as the weak overcoming the strong（柔弱胜强）, holding oneself aloof from worldly success（不争）, emptying the heart of desire（清心寡欲）, adopting an easy-going manner, retiring at the height of one's career（功成身退）, being selfless and modest, etc. have exerted great influence on the Chinese mind, and have been applied to politics, economy, military affairs, culture, business, and social intercourse. Chinese *jujitsu*（柔道）, traditional shadow boxing（太极拳） and quiescent *Qigong*（静气功） originate in the gist and spirit of Taoism.

Lao Zi（575 B.C.E.—? B.C.E.）, originally named Li Er（李耳）, styled Bo Yang（伯阳）, also called Lao Dan（老聃）, was the greatest philosopher and thinker in ancient China, as well as the founder of the school of thought—Taoism. According to Sima Qian's *Historical Records*, Lao Zi was born in Ku County（苦县） in the State of Chu（楚） and made curator of the imperial archives of Luoyang（周国都洛邑任藏室史，相当于今天的国

家档案馆馆长）.

Lao Zi is a legendary figure. It is said that he lived 160 years. His mother was pregnant for 81 years before he was born from her armpit. At birth, he already had white eyebrows and beard. He is twenty years older than Confucius who walked long distance to Luoyang to seek advice from him. Confucius said, "Lao Zi is still quite strong."

To Lao Zi, the search for fame and honor could only lead to perversion of the simplicity of human nature. So he resigned from office and returned to his old home. Yet, even at home, he was fed up with his aversion to curious visitors (Confucius included). Driven by an unceasing desire, to escape to the unknown, the aged philosopher decided upon his journey to the unknown. In a two-wheeled carriage drawn by black oxen, he set out to leave the deluded, society-corrupted world behind him. But at the western pass he was forbidden to go through the gate until he had written his philosophy. Lao Zi, thereupon, lingered in the gatehouse long enough to compose the treatise that came down to us as *Tao Te Ching* (《道德经》) or *Classics of the Tao and Its Power* in which he expounded his views in succinct, crisp sentences, some even obscure and cryptic. Then he departed over the pass, to be heard of no more.

Composed of 81 chapters, the book *Tao Te Ching* covers a wide range of subjects, from the law of universe, and heaven and earth, to the details of social phenomena, including man's thinking and the principle towards life. Among the immense amount of Chinese classics, two of them—*Lun Yu* (*Analects*) and *Dao De Jing* (*Tao Te Ching*) stand conspicuously, side by side, and make a significant impact upon the shaping and development of Chinese culture.

Taoism

Taoism is indigenous to China. Together with Confucianism, it has exerted great influence on the thinking of the Chinese people, as well as on the political, economic and cultural life of the country. In many ways, the doctrines of Confucianism and Taoism complement each other, running side by side like two powerful streams through later Chinese thought and literature. Contrary to the solemn, pompous gravity and burden of social responsibilities of Confucianism, Taoism advocates a carefree flight from the respectability and conventional duties of society. Whereas the Confucians were concerned about human and mundane affairs, the Taoists held out a vision of another, transcendental world of spirit. While the Confucians tried to find the secrets of life in men and their better relationships, the Taoists turned to nature for the secrets of life. Whereas the Confucian classics are often prosaic and dull, moralistic and commonsensical, the early Taoist writings are all wit and paradox, mysticism and poetic vision. Developing as two streams of thought in later ages, Confucianism is practised by officials and scholars in their offices and studies, trying to be good family men, conscientious officials and sober, responsible citizens, while Taoism is pursued by those who are in their private chambers or mountain retreats, seeking to get rid of the cares of official life and the agonies in social experience.

The Taoist writings have rendered a leaven of poetry and mysticism to Chinese literature and thought, without which they would be a much poorer and shallower affair. The ancient Chinese thinkers wished to give an explanation for the evident harmony and order in nature as a whole. This was due to the concept which they arrived at—the *Tao*. The harmony and orderliness displayed in heaven and earth were the results of the cosmic presence of the *Tao*. Literally, the word *Tao* means "a way" or "a road." Sometimes it denotes the "channel" of a river. In general, it means "the way to go." It includes the standard procedure of things, the correct method of their operation and behavior.

The *Tao* is described as existing before the universe came into being, an unchanging principle, and the mother of all things. It images the forefathers of the Lord. It is the natural way as well as the human way, a model for human behavior. This way of nature's functioning has been a way of perfection. The *Tao* is emphatically a way of harmony, integration and cooperation. Its natural tendency is towards peace, prosperity and health. If the *Tao* were ever to be followed everywhere, heaven, mankind, and the earth would form a single, harmonious unit, with every part cooperating towards universal well-being.

The Taoist philosophy has rich contents, yet it may be summed up in two points:

Wuwei（无为）

The Taoists hold that contemplation of the universe will lead to the discovery of the nameless first principle, and to the disposition that should accompany such contemplation, and indeed the whole of life. This disposition is expressed by the term "*Wuwei*." Literally, it means "non-action." In fact, it does not signify the absence of action, but rather acting without artificiality, without over-action, without attachment to action itself. In other words, it means quietude, non-aggression, and non-meddlesome action. We have already come to the practical part of Taoism—the way of living according to the way（顺其自然）.

This, at first glance, seems negative, but it is not quite so. There is affirmation in the quietism of *Wuwei*; its attendant virtues in human life are kindness, sincerity and humanity. If one does not meddle with others, human relations will fall naturally and simply. There will be a spontaneous birth of true love, real kindness, simplicity, and contentment in the lives and relationships of men, as the restraint of self from anger, ambition and meddlesome action is never negative in its consequences.

Wuwei is a state of mind as well as a cardinal principle towards life.

As a state of mind, it aims to achieve peace and quietness of mind. To attain such a disposition, the Taoists advocate *Zuowang*（坐忘）, or sitting and forgetting, in other words, fasting of the mind. This requires emptying of the senses and the mind itself. Emptiness is the fasting of the mind. In this way, it is said, you can find absolute happiness, and cast away all the agonies and annoyances of life.

Wuwei is also the cardinal principle of the Taoists towards life. Do not allow outside things to entangle one's self, let events take their natural course, adopt an easy-going and un-forceful manner, and follow the way of life according to the Way.

It is the Taoist view that the wise man who has acquired the secret of good life "follows the inevitable" and "simply moves with things".

Te（德）, or power of morality, or power for good

It is the power of naturalness, of simplicity, even of weakness. Yet, it teaches of survival, of how to keep one's own integrity in the time of disorder. This is possibly the most important point in the Taoist philosophy, and has immense influence on the development of Taoist religion. We could understand this Taoist teaching better by quoting some sayings from *Tao Te Ching*:

> The highest good is like water.
>
> Water benefits all things generously without striving with them.
>
> Staying in the lowly place that men disdain,
>
> It is close to the Tao.
>
> It knows to keep to the ground in choosing the dwelling.
>
> It knows to hide in the hidden deep in cultivating the mind.
>
> It knows to be gentle and kind in dealing with others.
>
> It knows to keep its words in speaking.
>
> It knows to maintain order in governing.
>
> It knows to be efficient in handling business.
>
> It knows to choose the right moment in making a move.
>
> Since it does not strive with others,
>
> It is free from blame.

【原文】

上善若水，水善利万物而不争。处众人之所恶，故几于道。

居善地，心善渊，与善仁，言善信，正善治，事善能，动善时。

夫唯不争，故无尤。

【今译】

最高的善行，就像水一样。水滋养万物而不与其相争。它处于人们厌恶的洼地，所以能接近于"道"。

居住懂得选择地方，心地善于深沉，待人坚持仁爱，说话坚持诚信，施政善于治理，办事讲究效率，行动会择时机。

唯与人不争，所以没有罪过。

The cardinal principle of the Taoists towards life is based upon the belief that "All things run the cycle." "Returning is the motion of the *Tao*." "All things go back to their common origin; ultimately they blend into one." The process of reversion and return is universal and constant in all things. All natural process is marked by the sameness of coming into being (birth), reaching maturity and reverting to non-being (death).

The Taoists believed that "Things turn to their opposite when they reach the extreme"（物极必反）. Just as Lao Zi said, "Good fortune lies within bad, bad fortune lurks within good.（祸兮福所依，福兮祸所伏）" That is, opposites exist in all things. The opposites within a thing do not remain unchanged. It is an invariable law in things that if any movement goes to its extreme of development, it necessarily has to execute a return.

Some Epigrams and Wise Sayings by Lao Zi

少则得，多则感。

Have little and you will gain,

Have much and you will be misled.

夫唯不争，故天下莫能与之争。

He who does not strive with anyone,

Is invincible.

知人者智，自知者明。

He who knows others is clever,

He who knows himself has insight.

将欲夺之，必固与之。

What is to be despoiled in the end,

Is richly endowed at first.

天下难事，必作于易；天下大事，必作于细。

Difficult things can only be tackled when they are easy,

Big things can only be achieved by attending to their small beginnings.

合抱之木，生于毫末；九层之台，起于累土；千里之行，始于足下。

A tree as big as a man's embrace springs from a tiny sprout,

A tower nine stories high begins with a heap of earth,

A journey of a thousand li starts from where you stand.

祸莫大于轻敌。

There is no greater calamity than to under–estimate the strength of your enemy.

哀者胜矣。

Victory belongs to the grieving side.

天网恢恢，疏而不漏。

Vast and sparse–meshed as the Heaven's net is,

Yet nothing can slip through it.

民不畏死，奈何以死惧之？

When the people are no longer afraid of death,

Why scare them with the threat of death?

信言不美，美言不信。

Sincere words are not sweet,

Sweet words are not sincere.

见素抱朴，少私寡欲。

See the Simple and embrace the Primal,

Diminish the Self and curb the Desire!

人法地，地法天，天法道，道法自然。

Man follows the ways of the earth,

The earth follows the way of Heaven,

Heaven follows the ways of Tao.

Tao follows its own ways.

轻则失本，躁则失君。

To be light is to be separated from one's root,

To be restless is to lose one's self—mastery.

知其荣，守其辱，天下为谷。

Know the glories,

Keep to the lowly,

And be the Fountain of the World.

师之所处，荆棘生焉。大军之后，必有凶年。

Wherever armies are stationed, thorny bushes grow.

After a great war, bad years invariably follow.

贵以贱为本，高以下为基。

Humility is the root, from which greatness springs,

And the low is the foundation from which the high is built.

反者道之动，弱者道之用。

The movement of the Tao consists in Returning,

The use of the Tao consists in softness.

大方无隅，大器晚成。

Great squareness has no corners.

Great talents ripen late.

知足不辱，知止不殆，可以长久。

To know when you have enough is to be immune from disgrace.

To know when to stop is to be preserved from perils.

Only thus can you endure long.

祸莫大于不知足，咎莫大于欲得。

There is no greater calamity than not knowing to be content.

There is no bigger evil than covetousness.

知者不言，言者不知。

He who knows does not speak.

He who speaks does not know.

以正治国，以奇用兵。

Govern a kingdom by normal rules,

Fight a war by exceptional moves.

重积德则无不克。

To have a double reserve of Virtue is to overcome everything.

治大国若烹小鲜。

Ruling a big kingdom is like cooking a small fish.

美言可以市尊，美行可以加人。

A good word will find its own market.

A good deed may be used as a gift to another.

江海所以能为百谷王者，以其善下之。

How does the sea become the king of all streams?

Because it lies lowest.

天之道，利而不害；圣人之道，为而不争。

The Way of Heaven is to benefit, not to harm.

The Way of the Sage is to do his duty, not to strive with anyone.

· Seminar ·

Comment on the philosophy of Lao Zi and Zhuang Zi.

Taoism as a Religion

As a religion, Taoism was first known as the Five Piculs of Rice Sect（五斗米道），

founded in the Eastern Han Dynasty (25 A.D.—220 A.D.) in the Heming Mountains in Sichuan Province. The Taoists made Lao Zi their supreme god, taking *Tao Te Ching* as their cannon, with Zhang Daoling (张道陵), the founder, as the Sect's Heavenly Teacher (天师).

Together with Buddhism, it has had a great impact on the thinking of the Chinese people, as well as on the political, economic and cultural life of the country. Even today we can still find traces of its influence among the Chinese people. For instance, the idiom "Like the Eight Immortals crossing the sea, each displaYing his / her special prowess (八仙过海，各显神通)" has its origin in the Taoist fairy tale "The Eight Immortals Crossing the Sea." Many people still worship the God of Wealth (财神), called Marshal Zhao (赵公元帅), in hope of achieving a big fortune and put the portrait of the God of the Door (门神) on the door, which is supposed to keep away demons.

Taoism has a god for almost everything—the sun, moon, stars, wind, rain, thunder, lightning, mountains, rivers and the country. The religion also has gods of the Town, Land, Kitchen, Door and Wealth. The God of the Kitchen (灶神) is believed to be in charge of every household's fortune and misfortune. It is said that every year, on the 23rd day of the 12th month of the lunar year, the Kitchen God ascends to Heaven to report to the Jade Emperor (玉帝) on the good and evil of the household in which he dwells and comes back on the Spring Festival Eve. That's why people burn incense (烧香) on the 23rd day of the 12th month of the lunar year, for the purpose of sending the Kitchen God to Heaven, and let off firecrackers and fireworks on the Spring Festival Eve to welcome him back.

After a brilliant beginning, Taoism was gradually appropriated by those who wandered off in search of the secret of eternal life, which led them into such a slough of superstitions that they eventually lost credit in the eyes of the intellectual class. As the later Taoists built their doctrines on ancient witchcraft and recipes for immortality, absorbing all sorts of popular superstitions and demon lore, the Taoist school became more and more a cult of popular religion and later, an object of ridicule among the educated people.

Zhuang Zi

Zhuang Zi and His Philosophy

Zhuang Zi (庄子) is the second great figure of the early Taoist school which is known as the "philosophy of Lao Zi and Zhuang Zi (老庄哲学)" in the history of Chinese culture. The book, bearing his name, is probably a combination of his own essays and those of his disciples and imitators. It is one of the most witty and imaginative works of all Chinese literature. Like

Lao Zi, it does not depend upon methodical arguments for its effect, but upon the use of parable and allegory, paradox and fanciful imagination. Let's quote some lines from his work to illustrate this point.

> Once upon a time, Zhuang Zhou dreamed that he became a butterfly, fluttering about with enjoyment, not knowing that he was Zhuang Zhou. Suddenly he awoke with a start. Bewildered, he did not know whether he was the butterfly in the dream or a butterfly dreaming that he was Zhuang Zhou. There must be some distinction between Zhuang Zhou and the butterfly. This is called the alternation of things.

【原文】

昔者庄周梦为蝴蝶，栩栩然蝴蝶也，自喻适志与！不知周也。俄然觉，则蘧蘧然周也。不知周之梦为蝴蝶与，蝴蝶之梦为周与？周与蝴蝶，则必有分矣。此之谓物化。

【今译】

从前庄周梦见自己变成蝴蝶，翩翩起舞，非常惬意，不知道自己是庄周了。忽然惊醒，愣愣怔怔的一个庄周！不知道是庄周梦中变成蝴蝶，还是蝴蝶梦中变成了庄周。蝴蝶和庄周，那么一定是有区别的了。这就叫作事物的转化。

Such an abstruse principle of philosophy, the alternation of things, was explained clearly by Zhuang Zi through telling a paradox. A thing is itself at a certain moment and something else at another moment. A man is a man at present and a pile of earth after death. Man cannot jump into the same river for the objective conditions have changed. Zhuang Zi used a simple story to express his philosophical view—nothing remains unchanged.

Zhuang Zi shares with Lao Zi the central concept of *Tao* as the principle underlying and governing all existence. However, he is not so much concerned with the *Tao* as a guide to life but as a way to transcend human life, which has a supreme value in itself. A philosophy of acceptance, Lao Zi teaches the Way of the world and the virtues of survival: humility, gentleness and non-striving. Zhuang Zi, on the other hand, is indifferent to human society. He seeks neither to reform things nor to keep them as they are, but to rise above them. The text of Zhuang Zi makes an ardent plea for spiritual freedom: not the freedom of the individual from social conventions and restraints, but rather a self-transcending liberation from the limitation of one's own mind—from one's self-interested tendencies and prejudices.

Zhuang Zi's central concern may be described as the finding of absolute happiness of transcending the distinction between one's self and the universe by perfect union with the *Tao*. Zhuang Zi mentioned in essays the practice of "sitting and forgetting", that is, emptying the senses and fasting the mind:

> Let your ears and your eyes communicate with what is inside... Then even gods and spirits will come to dwell.

Zhuang Zi's ultimate view is a mystical one. According to Zhuang Zi, the true man is the one who comprehends and lives in the underlying unity of the *Tao*, who has achieved a happiness that is beyond all changes, a life that is beyond life and death. By a superior wisdom, the sage is no longer affected emotionally by the changes of this world. He has not lost sensibility, but has risen above it. To him, death is nothing more than a necessary and proper correlative of human life, the natural and desirable step following life, the rest after labor, the cure of the sickness in life.

Such is the vision of Zhuang Zi, boldly imaginative in asserting the freedom of the individual to seek his own fulfillment. Its subtlety and profundity continued to captivate the Chinese mind and induced others later to attempt a re-conciliation between the lofty view of Zhuang Zi and the problems of society.

III

Buddhism

The coming of Buddhism to China from India was a great event in the development of Chinese culture and of Buddhism itself. After a long period of assimilation, it established itself as a major system of thought as well as a religious practice, contributing greatly to the enrichment of Chinese philosophy and exercising an enduring influence on the Chinese popular religion and on the mind and character of the Chinese people. Indeed, it becomes one of the Three Pillars (Confucianism, Taoism and Buddhism) of the traditional culture of China.

The Buddhist religion was founded by Prince Siddhartha, son of King Suddhodana (Pure Rice King) of Kapilavastu (a town in the plains region of the modern Nepal-India border), between the 6th and 5th centuries B.C.E. Prince Siddhartha was also known as Sakyamuni（释迦牟尼） which Means "the wise man of the Sakya clan." He had given away the luxurious royal life and meditated under the pipal tree and had become Buddha （佛祖）, the founder of Buddhism.

Buddhism was introduced into the region inhabited by the Han people around the 1st century. According to historical records, during the reign of Emperor Aidi（汉哀帝）of the

Western Han Dynasty, in 2 B.C.E., an envoy named Yin Cun from Indoscy the went to Chang'an (Today's Xi'an) to impart Buddhist sutras to a Chinese scholar named Jing Lu (景卢). Emperor Mingdi (汉明帝) of the Eastern Han Dynasty later sent a mission to the Western Regions for Buddhist scriptures. He also had a temple built in Luoyang, known as the White Horse Temple, which was the first Buddhist temple in China. During the Wei and Jin Dynasties the influence of Buddhism spread widely.

The Buddhist doctrines eventually became integrated with traditional Chinese ethics and religious concepts. *Xuan Xue* (玄学, metaphysics) was very popular among the ruling classes at that time. The Buddhist doctrines had many things in common with *Xuan Xue*, and the two soon became one. During the Southern and Northern Dynasties the ruling classes further helped the spread of Buddhism by building temples and monasteries, translating Buddhist sutras and constructing grottoes, and many famous monks, scholars and teachers emerged. By the Sui and Tang Dynasties, Buddhism reached its apex of popularity and splendour, and different sects of Buddhism had been formed in China. Over a long period, Buddhism gradually took root in the feudal society of China, intermingling with Confucian and Taoist thought. It had a strong popular appeal and its ideas made a notable impact on Chinese philosophy, literature and art.

The most famous Buddhist grottoes remaining today are Mogao Grottoes of Dunhuang (敦煌莫高窟), Longmen Grottoes of Luoyang (洛阳龙门窟) and Yungang Grottoes of Datong (大同云冈窟). Among the other famous temples are: Shao Lin Temple in Henan Province (河南少林寺), Ci'en Temple in Xi'an (西安慈恩寺), Lingyin Temple in Hangzhou (杭州灵隐寺), etc.

The long history of Chinese Buddhism produced many famous monks, such as Fa Xian (法显), Xuan Zang (玄奘) and Jian Zhen (鉴真), who were also famous as travelers, scholars and legendary heroes.

Generally the Buddhist doctrines encompass three points: The world is impermanent and will eventually be destroyed; everything in the world is unreal; and the ultimate aim of a person's life is eternal tranquility. (三法印：诸行无常；诸法无我；涅槃寂静。)

The fundamental truths on which Buddhism is founded are not metaphysical or theological, but rather psychological. Its basic doctrine is the "four noble truths": life is inevitably full of sorrow; sorrow is due to craving; sorrow can only be stopped by the stopping of craving; and this can only be done by a course of a carefully disciplined and moral life, a life of concentration and meditation led by the Buddhist monks. (四圣谛：苦、集、灭、道。)

These four truths are the common property of all schools of Buddhist thought.

Thus the Buddha's last words might be translated: "Growing old is the dharma of all composites." (The word "dharma" is strictly untranslatable in English. Besides meaning "law" or "doctrine", it represents phenomena, and their qualities and characteristics.)

All things are composite, and as a corollary of this, all things are transient, for the composition of all aggregates is liable to change with time. Moreover, being essentially transient, they have no eternal Self or Soul, no abiding individuality. And, as we have seen, they are inevitably liable to sorrow. This three-fold characterization of the nature of the world and all that it contains—sorrow, transience, and soullessness—are frequently repeated in Buddhist literature.

· *Homework* ·

Write an essay about 1,000 words on Buddhism.

IV
Mo Zi and Moism

Mo Zi

Among the pre-Qin "hundred philosophers" was Mo Zi(墨子), who devoted his life selflessly to the welfare of the people and society.

Mo Zi (479 B.C.E.—381 B.C.E.) was born a few years after Confucius's death and died a few years before Mencius's birth. Some scholars held that the surname "Mo" had the implication of a form of punishment, or a kind of hard life, for in all his life Mo Zi lived a life no better than that of prisoners and slaves.

Mo Zi had an important place in the history of Chinese culture. Although Moism did not hold this position for long, its founder and his teachings left an indelible impression on the Chinese mind.

The core of Moism is universal love(兼爱), close to the assertion that "all men are equal before God." In his life time, rulers of the feudal states, to satisfy their endless material needs, sought after aggressive wars of annexation at the sacrifice of their weak neighbors, thus bringing the people into disastrous impasse. Mo Zi, standing by the common people, claimed the right of survival for the people and the weak and small states. He advocated economy and thrift. He condemned all forms of ritual, extravagant funerals, expensive entertainment, and offensive warfare, which would deteriorate the feeding, clothing and housing of the common people.

In denial of the cruel rulers, Mo Zi embraced his own social ideal and put forward the idea that "exaltation of the worthy (尚贤) is the foundation of good government," because "when the ignorant and the mean govern the wise and the noble, there is disorder." He emphasized the exaltation of the worthy and the employment of the capable (尚贤用能). The worthy should be exalted, promoted, enriched and honored, and made governors and officials.

In order to draw people's attention to his political claims and realize his social ideal, Mo Zi, on the one hand, sought after the thread of God and spirits; on the other, emphasized the unceasing efforts to improve oneself. Believing in Heaven as an active power manifesting love for all men, he stressed that men followed Heaven in this by practising universal love.

Mo Zi was a rigorist who set the most exacting standards for himself and his followers. In trying to gain acceptance for his principles, he drove himself tirelessly and unmercifully. He was ready to preach his gospel to anyone who would listen. At times, upon hearing the plans of a state to make war, he would hasten to dissuade the ruler from perpetrating such a crime. It is said that on one of these peace missions he walked ten days and ten nights, tearing off pieces of his garments to bind up his sore feet. Often, failing in his efforts at conciliation, Mo Zi and his followers would rush to aid in the defense of the state being attacked, gaining a reputation for their high skill in siege operation. In this way they became a tight knit and highly-disciplined group, leading an ascetic life.

Mo Zi is much more admired for his nobility of soul revealed in his service to others than his literary style which is plain and simple. His essays, varied as they appear, are not flowery yet sincere and expressive; his arguments, step by step, are logical and forceful.

V
Han Fei Zi and Legalism

Among the classical schools of thought in the period of the Warring States, Legalism was comparatively late in securing its theoretical position, yet it had tremendous influence upon the political life of its time. While the "vain" talks of Confucianism and Moism were refused one by one by the feudal lords, Legalism was accepted by the rulers of the feudal

Han Fei Zi

states since its appearance, and put into practice with great success.

Legalism was a very strict and stern philosophy. In its earliest form, it was probably the outgrowth of a need for a more rational organization of society and resources so as to strengthen the state against its rivals. This was to be accomplished by concentrating power in the hands of a single ruler and by the adoption of political institutions affording greater centralized control. Guan Zhong（管仲）, a legalist in the seventh century B.C.E., worked to make Qi the strongest state of his time by increasing the power of the ruler.

As the struggle among the Warring States became more intense, rulers were no longer interested in the vain talks of humanity and righteousness and the examples of the ancient sage-kings. There came forward a group of technicians of power who put the state and its interests ahead of all human and moral concerns and glorified the power of the king for the sake of the survival of the country.

The outstanding representative of this school was Shang Yang（商鞅）(d. 338 B.C.E.), prime minister of Qin, who was the original organizer of the state's long drive to imperial power. He put forward a series of policies known in history as the "Shang Yang Reform" and successfully employed them to make Qin possess the sweeping strength among the feudal states. He completely rejected the traditional virtue of humanity and righteousness which the Confucians had urged upon rulers, denying that such lofty ideals had any practical relationship to the hard realities of political life. He advocated war as a means of strengthening the power of the ruler, expanding the territory and making the people disciplined and submissive. He conceived of a political order in which all old feudal divisions of power would be swept away and all authority reside in one central administration headed by an absolute monarchy. The state would be ordered by an exhaustive set of laws defining in detail the duties and responsibilities of all its members. Severe punishments would restrain evil while generous rewards would encourage what was beneficial to the strength and well-being of the state. Agriculture, as the basis of the economy, would be promoted intensively while commerce and intellectual endeavor were to be severely restricted as non-essential and diversionary. The people would live a frugal and obedient life devoted to the interests of the state in war and peace.

Another outstanding representative of this school was Li Si（李斯, d. 208 B.C.E.）who assisted King Cheng of Qin in its annexation of the other six feudal states. By utilizing Legalist centralization of power, regimentation of its people and aggressive warfare, King Cheng built himself up to a position of forbidding strength in the late years of the Zhou Dynasty and finally succeeded in swallowing up the last of its rivals and uniting all of China. In 221 B.C.E., King Cheng assumed the title of Qin Shihuang (the First Emperor of Qin) and Li Si became prime minister of the new empire. Thus, for the first time, one of the schools of classical thought had its teachings adopted as the orthodox philosophy of a regime ruling all of China.

At Li Si's urging, the First Emperor carried out a series of sweeping changes and innovations that, in the course of a few years, radically affected the entire structure of Chinese life and society. One of these was the complete abolition of all feudal ranks and privileges and the disarmament of all individuals. The entire area of China was brought under the direct control of the central government through an administrative system of prefectures and counties. With this unification of the nation came measures for the standardization of weights, measures and writing script, the destruction of all barriers between districts, and the construction of better roads and communications. Wars were undertaken to subdue neighboring peoples and expand the borders of the nation; masses of people were forcibly moved to new areas for the purpose of defense or resettlement, and labor gangs were set to work constructing the Great Wall out of small defensive walls of the old feudal states.

The most outstanding representative of the Legalist school was Han Fei (d. 233 B.C.E.) who, though not a successful politician, left us an excellent statement on the theoretical basis of this school. He came from the royal house of the state of Han. He was a student of the Confucian Xun Zi, who, as we know, taught that human nature is evil. In 234 B.C.E., on a mission to Qin, sent by the King of Han, Han Fei was favorably received at the Qin court but eventually met his death through the machinations of his fellow student, Li Si. His writings were collected into the book *Han Fei Zi*, composed of 55 essays. In him all previous teachings of the Legalist thinkers were synthesized and brought to their higher development.

In his essays he explicitly expounded the principal ideas of the Legalist school, which, to a large extent, were put into practice by the rulers of the State of Qin. He held that history is progressing. It is an inevitable law that the new social system will replace the old. So any social system and government policy must be renewed in accord with the changed situation. In his famous essay *The Five Vermin of the State* (《五蠹》), he said, "Hence the sage does not seek to follow the ways of the ancients, nor does he regard precedents as the rule. He examines the circumstances of his own time and plans his course of action accordingly." （是以圣人不期修古，不法常可；论世之事，因为之备。） He ridiculed those who adhered to the ways of ancient sage-kings were just like the man who kept watch at the tree stump, in the vain hope of getting another hare.

It should be noticed that, in their complete rejection of the ethical values of Confucianism, in their emphasis upon government by law rather than by individual leadership, and in their scorn for the ideals and examples of the past, the Legalists represent the exact antithesis of Confucian thinking. Yet, the Legalists had obviously learned something from both the Moists and the Taoists. Mo Zi's stress on uniform standards and on the mobilization of society for the achievement of utilitarian ends was strongly echoed in the totalitarian aims of the Legalists, although they obviously had no use for Mo Zi's doctrine of universal love and his condemnation of offensive warfare. Moreover, Lao Zi's old idea of non-action as a way of government was applied to the Legalist conception of the ideal ruler, who, took no direct part in the government but served as a semi-divine figurehead while the elaborate legal machinery of government functioned of its own accord. The ruler could retire to dwell in the midst of his deep palace, far removed from the eyes of the populace, enjoying the luxuries and sensual delights appropriate to his exalted position.

It is obvious that there is a strong anti-intellectualism in the system of Legalist thought. Han Fei ranked the intellectuals among the five vermin of the state to be wiped out from society when he said, "This then is the customary experience of a disorderly state: the learned men will exalt the ways of the early kings and make a show of humanity and righteousness. They will adorn their manners and clothes and embroider their arguments and speeches so as to scatter doubts on the law of the age and beguile the mind of the sovereign. The itinerant speakers will advocate deceptive theories and utilize foreign influence to accomplish their selfish purposes, being unmindful of the benefit of the state." （是故乱国之俗：其学者，则称先王之道以籍仁义，盛容服而饰辩说，以疑当世之法，而贰人主之心；其言谈者，为设诈称，借于外力，以成其私，而遗社稷之利。——《韩非子：五蠹》）

At the suggestion of Han Fei, the First Emperor of Qin gave orders that all books in the imperial archives, save the memoirs of Qin, be burned; all persons in the empire, except members of the Academy of Learned Scholars, in possession of the *Book of Odes*, the *Book of History*, and the discourses of the hundred philosophers should be taken to the local governors and indiscriminately burned; those who dared to talk to each other about the *Book of Odes* and the *Book of History* should be executed and their bodies be exposed in the market place; anyone who referred to the past to criticize the present should be put to death; officials who failed to report cases that had come under their attention were equally guilty; those who had not destroyed the forbidden books thirty days after the decree was issued were to be branded and sent to build the Great Wall. As a result, all books except those on medicine and pharmacy, divination by the tortoise shells and milfoil, and agriculture and arboriculture, were burned and four hundred alleged Confucian scholars were buried alive. This was known in history as "the burning of books and the burying of Confucian scholars."

It is interesting to know that the three representatives of Legalism, each saw the height of his glory, all met with violent death. The harsh policies they employed on others to win their political success were employed on themselves. Shang Yang was finally executed by his political enemy and his corpse was disintegrated by the pulling of five horses. After the death of the First Emperor, Li Si and Zhao Gao, by concealing the death of the emperor and forging orders in his name, had succeeded in destroying their rivals and seizing control of the government. The Second Emperor became a helpless puppet, cut off in the depths of the palace from all contact with no information from the outside world. Then Zhao Gao turned on Li Si and destroyed him and his family, using against him the very Legalist methods that Li Si had employed. Han Fei, as we know, was persecuted by his fellow student Li Si under false charges.

· Seminar ·
1. What is the core of Moism?
2. Tell what you know about Legalism.

VI
Four Books and Five Classics

Four Books
The Great Learning(《大学》)
The Great Learning is a brief essay of some 1,750 words. Its Chinese title, *Da Xue*, means education for the adult or higher education. It has been variously attributed to Zi Si (子思), Confucius's grandson, and Confucius's disciple Zeng Zi (曾子), or to one of his disciples. Some scholars, however, especially in the last three decades, have dated it as late as 200 B.C.E. In all likelihood its basic ideas go back to Confucius, though the essay itself definitely belongs to a later age.

The central theme of the work is self-cultivation. This is, however, no ordinary guide to self-improvement for an individual, but rather seeks to establish the value of self-cultivation in terms of social ends, showing its relevance to the problem of good government. Indeed, the argumentation here often makes sense only if we understand that it is addressed to the ruler and its officials, rather than to any ordinary man in search for moral guidance. Before a man can regulate and discipline others, he must learn to regulate and discipline himself. To accomplish this, *The Great Learning* offers a method or a goal which became famous as the "three programs" and "eight points" (三纲八条目):

The way of *The Great Learning* lies in illustrating value, rejuvenating the people, and reaching perfection. The ancients who wish to illustrate virtue throughout the world would first govern well their own state. To govern their state well, they would first regulate their families. To regulate their families, they would first cultivate their own personality. To cultivate their personality, they would rectify their minds. To rectify their minds, they would first strive to be sincere in their thoughts. Wishing for sincerity in their thoughts, they would expand their knowledge. The expansion of knowledge lay in the investigation of things.

Broad in scope and rather general in meaning, these three programs: illustrating value (明德), rejuvenating people (亲民) and reaching perfection (止于至善) and eight points: investigation of thing (格物), expansion of knowledge (至知), sincerity in thoughts (正心), rectification of minds (诚意), cultivation of personality (修身), regulation of the family (齐家), government of the state (治国), illustration of virtue throughout the world (平天下) seemed to outline, in neat and concise form, a complete system of education and social organization, which has a tremendous and ever-lasting influence on later generation not only in China, but also in Japan, Korea and elsewhere in the Chinese cultural sphere. Especially in Neo-Confucian thought the interpretation of the "three programs" and "eight points" became one of the central issues of philosophy and ethics.

The Doctrine of the Mean (《中庸》)

The Doctrine of the Mean is a treatise on the golden mean of the Confucian school. It further develops the idea that "excess is the just as bad as deficiency", ranks neutrality the optimal yardstick for morality and conduct and puts forward the pre-requisites and methods for practising and achieving the way of Mean.

What Heaven bestows on us is called Nature; to accord with this Nature is called the Way; the training of this Way is called Instruction. Since the Mean is Nature, it is naturally connected with the Way and Instruction.

Before pleasure, anger, sorrow and joy are evoked, the mind is in a state called "neutrality." When these feelings awaken and each reaches its due degree, it is called the state of harmony. This state of neutrality is the great root of all existence while that of harmony is the far-reaching way. Once neutrality and harmony exist in perfection, Heaven and Earth will take their proper place and all things will be nourishing and flourishing.

A man of virtue abides by the Mean while a villain acts against it. The Mean of a man of virtue lies in neutrality all the time; the Mean of a villain lies in being without scruple. The virtue of Mean may be the earliest rule of conduct, which is generally difficult to practise.

It is hard to fully abide by the principle of the Mean. Both excess and deficiency have departed from the Mean. The wise over-do it while the stupid under-do it; a man of virtue goes beyond it while a villain fails to comprehend it.

The Doctrine of the Mean is comprehensive and detailed. Though it appears abstruse where it is profound, it is embedded in ordinary things. *The Doctrine of the Mean* is nothing of mysteries, nor is it far from human beings. Those who practise the Way and render it mysterious have not achieved the Way—you should not give what you do not want others to give you. *The Doctrine of the Mean* contains four guiding principles: sons waiting upon fathers; subjects upon monarchies; young brothers upon elders; helping friends before getting help from them. All this can be achieved by heeding what one says and does.

The Mean also lies in the change of conduct in accordance with the changes in one's situations. Only in this way can one be carefree and content.

The practice of the Mean primarily lies in sincerity. Confucius once said, "Sincerity is the Way of Heaven; the attainment of sincerity is the Way of man. Sincerity has no limits. It is the beginning and end of all things. Therefore a man of virtue regards sincerity as the most precious value. Only those who have sincerity can create the permanent rule of the world, establish the perfect Mean and possess the virtue of *Ren* and profound thoughts."

The Doctrine of the Mean was written during the period of time from the pre-Qin era to the beginning of the Han Dynasty when the feudal ideology began to take shape. The philosophy of the Mean as conveyed in the book and other Confucian ideas constituted an important part of the super-structure of the feudal society. *The Doctrine of the Mean*, taken out from *The Book of Rites* as an independent chapter and then edited into *The Four Books*, was the textbook of feudal ideology, exerting a tremendous influence upon later generations.

The Confucian Analects (《论语》)

The Confucian Analects, or simply *Analects*, a question-and-answer record of the conversations between Confucius and his disciples, is the first and most important treatise of Confucianism and carries the major teachings of the ancient Chinese master.

As a gem with defects in the Chinese heritage, *Analects* has, for more than two thousand years, exerted tremendous influence on the Chinese politics and culture.

Mencius (《孟子》)

Mencius, a book written by Mencius's disciples to record the words and deeds of the master and his students, is the cornerstone of Neo-Confucianism after Confucius.

Since the Han Dynasty, the teachings of Mencius had won increasing influence and Mencius himself enjoyed such a privileged position as to be revered as "second only to the Sage (Confucius)."

Regarding the people as the basis of a state, Mencius advocates for "humane, or benevolent government." By "humane government," the master means that the feudal ownership system should remain while allowing the possession of some properties by the people, that land should be leased to the people who shall support the rules while maintaining their own living, that efforts should be mad to relieve the people by "sparing the use of punishments and fines and reducing taxes and levies", and that a ruler should think in others' shoes. Mencius holds that, with benevolent, a feudal ruler can remain at ease.

While emphasizing *Ren* (benevolence), Mencius attaches great importance to *Yi* (righteousness). In his eyes, whatever complies with *Ren* is *Yi*, for "*Ren* is a safe shelter, *Yi* the right path." Everyone should nurture *Ren* and practise *Yi*, without which a man is "inhuman."

The Mencius's doctrine of *Ren* and *Yi* stems from his belief in the goodness of human nature. Mencius was sure that man has a prior goodness, which is an inborn trait of personality. Idealistic as it may sound, Mencius's theory of the goodness of human nature indicates the good wishes of the ancient master, who expected all humans to follow what is good.

The resourceful Mencius was a highly accomplished philosopher and man of letters. His writings are fluent, incisive and powerful. For this reason, even though *Mencius* mainly consists of recorded utterances, as does *Analects*, the former is artistically much more successful than the latter.

Five Classics

I-Ching (*Book of Changes*《易经》)

▼ What Kind of Book Is *I-Ching* ▲

Some people understand that since *I-Ching* is a book of divination, it goes without saying that it is a book of fetishes and superstitions. Then, why has it been studied since it took its form in the dawn of history? What is the true essence of this book? What can we learn from it?

Beginning as a book of court oracles (占卜), deep in meaning when ethical values were attached to the oracle announcements (卦辞), it became a book of wisdom, a book of history, a book of philosophy, a book of poetry, a book dealing with the universal laws of the development of things, eventually one of the five classics of Confucianism, and provided the common source for both Confucian and Taoist philosophy. It is one of the first efforts of the human mind to place itself within the universe (天人合一). It has exerted a living influence in China for three thousand years, and interest in it has been spreading in the West. The Taoists bypassed its text altogether and lay emphasis on the symbolism of the hexagrams alone, building a numerological system (数字占卦术) akin to astrology, which became the dominant influence in Chinese folk culture and still touches the daily lives of millions of people in its life-nurturing practices and medical theory.

The Confucians claimed the *I-Ching* as their own and stuffed into its archaic and cryptic text a rigid moralistic interpretation known as the Ten Wings (十翼). In fact, the stilted prose of the Ten Wings bore no relation to the spirit and substance of the original *I-Ching*.

In short, the text of *I-Ching* is a compilation of divination texts, containing folk poetry that still rhymes in modern Chinese, and historical tales that are still part of the living folklore of the Chinese people. On closer examination, we can find an underlying philosophy. The Taoist invocation (祷文) of a magic numerology is a tangential exercise independent of the original *I-Ching*. The systematic moralization of the Confucians is an act of vandalism in practice. The *I-Ching* is simply what it was originally meant to be—an oracle.

The central theme of this book is that all things run their cycles and no situation remains unchangeable. It offers hope in the depth of despair, and warns of destruction at the height of success. This is of course the philosophy of *Yin*, *Yang* and change.

The original text must have been compiled, weeded out and edited over a long period of time, guided by the empirical test of its effectiveness as oracle. The poetic voicing of an underlying philosophy must have been a form that emerged only after long evolution, as something essential in the making of a good oracle.

▼ How the Book *I-Ching* Came into Being? ◢

According to legends, an early sage (some say emperor), Fuxi (伏羲), observed the phenomena in Heaven and the developments of things on Earth, studied the languages of birds and beasts and the proper disposition of land, drew the lessons from persons near and things afar, and then created the eight trigrams (八卦) which are figures made up of three elements that are either *Yin* or *Yang*, symbolizing the basic elements of a recognizable universe: Heaven, Earth, Thunder, Water, Mountain, Wind, Fire and Lake.

Millennia passed. Legendary dynasties rose and fell. At the end of the Shang Dynasty, King Wen of the State of Zhou stacked the trigrams on top of one another, making sixty-four hexagrams (卦). Then, the oracle announcements of the hexagrams were annotated and embellished by Confucius, and Ten Wings was attached to it. That is the book *I-Ching* that came down to us.

▼ *Yin* and *Yang* ◢

According to some unknown Chinese philosophers as early as 1000 B.C.E., everything is constituted by the interplay of two modes of energy, *Yin* and *Yang*, and therefore has the characteristics of both. The *Yang* is described as masculine in character—active, warm, dry, bright, procreative and positive. It is seen in the sun, the fire, in anything with heat in it, in the southern side of a hill, in the northern side of a river, representing the male property of all kinds. The *Yin* is an energy-mode in a lower and slower key; it is the female or negative principle in nature, fertile and breeding, dark, cold, wet, secret and mysterious. It is seen in shadows, in quiescent things, in the north side of a hill and the south bank of a river. A single object may at one moment show *Yin* characteristics and at another become a *Yang* object aflame with energy. Thus a dried-out log is to all appearance *Yin* in character, but if put in a fire it will prove to have *Yang* qualities in abundance. This is not because its substance has altered, but because its inner activity has changed from one mode to another.

The Zhou people knew the deepest secret of the universe—that *Yin* and *Yang* are at the root of all things, and together in alternation they are the moving force of our world and all its manifestations.

The idea that anything can be described in terms of two basic elements is beautiful in its simplicity and forms the foundation from which the *I-Ching* was constructed.

▼ The Book of Oracles ◢

In early times, there were various types of divination. In the time of the Shang, a favorite method of divination was to scrape a thin spot on a tortoise shell, put it over a flame, and have diviners read the cracks that appeared on the shell. By the time of the Zhou Dynasty (after 1100 B.C.E.), these cracks were seen to conform to *Yin* and *Yang* lines found in the Ba Gua (八卦) or Eight Trigrams which are all the possible combinations of broken and unbroken lines arranged in sets of three. The unbroken line (——) was called the *Yang-Yao* (阳爻), because it was held to represent the male or positive principle; while the broken line (— —) was called *Yin-Yao* (阴爻) and represent the female or negative principle. The Eight Trigrams, arranged according to later tradition within an octagon with the *Yin-Yang* symbol in the center to represent creation (创世纪), looked like the figure below:

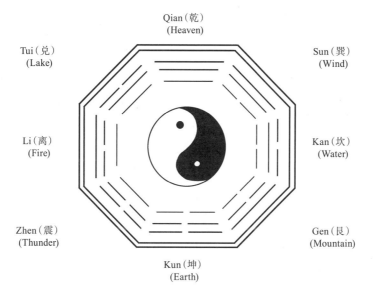

At the beginning, *I-Ching* was a collection of linear signs to be used as oracles, by putting together three lines, *Yin* or *Yang*, in all possible combinations to represent the eight basic elements:

HEAVEN	EARTH	THUNDER	WATER
MOUNTAIN	WIND	FIRE	LAKE

With these eight elements as building blocks, a higher level of representation was achieved by stacking trigrams upon trigrams, creating the sixty-four hexagrams.

Each hexagram has an opening text called "the judgement" (卦辞), and each of the six lines of a hexagram also has its own text (爻辞). The judgement describes the general idea of the hexagram as a whole, and the individual lines refer to specific elements in the development of the central idea. This structure renders both a general reading and a more specific assessment of the meanings of the moment. The hexagrams and the text together comprise the *I-Ching* which served as the court oracle of the Zhou Dynasty. The character *Yi* （易） means "change," and *Jing*（经）means "classic." In addition, the character *Yi* has other meanings, such as "simple" （for the natural law of Heaven and Earth is simple in nature）, and "not easy"（for the natural phenomena and the relations between man and nature, man and man are complicated and in constant flux, it is not easy to understand）. Yet, if we grasp their essence, it is quite simple. The concept of change comes from the basic nature of *Yin* and *Yang*, which are always changing into each other. When *Yin* holds sway for too long, it becomes old and renews itself by changing into *Yang*, and vice versa. When a given line in a hexagram changes, it turns the original hexagram into a new one. Thus each line has a dynamic quality, which drives the static hexagram into motion.

By associating a hexagram with a given moment in time or a particular human situation and by focusing on this dynamic aspect of the hexagram, we can derive a symbolic reading of the portents（潜势）. The changing, or "old" lines relate directly to the situation or question posed, and the hexagram that is created when these lines renew themselves indicates the direction of the changes. Thus the *I-Ching* assesses both the current moment and the dynamic forces of the future, already implicit in the present.

The specific text evolved as the *I-Ching* was formalized as a tool for divination, or oracle, but each hexagram expresses its own individual style. Sometimes it gives an omen; sometimes it tells a story or dispenses advice. It is full of historical references. The language has an austere poetic quality and the message conveyed by the text is often obscure, partly due to the archaic language, but mainly because these judgements were meant to be oracular pronouncements.

▼ The Book of Philosophy ◢

Of far greater significance than the use of *I-Ching* as an oracle is its other use, namely, as a book of wisdom. It is obvious that Lao Zi drew wisdom from this book, which inspired some of his profoundest aphorisms. Indeed, all his thoughts are permeated with its teachings. Confucius devoted himself to reflection upon it. He probably wrote down some of his interpretative comments and imparted orally to his pupils. The version that has come down to our time was edited and annotated by Confucius.

If we closely examine *I-Ching*, we can find a prevailing philosophy and some basically important concepts implied. The underlying idea of the whole is the idea of change. The theme is that *Yin* and *Yang* alternate in an unending sequence and that an extreme situation must change to make room for opposite elements. Nearly all the greatest and most significant philosophical thinking in the three thousand years of Chinese cultural history has taken its inspiration from this book. The two branches of Chinese philosophy, Confucianism and Taoism, have their common root here. In *Analects*, it is related that Confucius, standing by a river, said, "Everything flows on and on like this river, without pause, day and night." (逝者如斯夫，不舍昼夜。) This expresses the idea of change. Those who have perceived the meaning of change fix his attention no longer on transitory individual things but on the unchangeable, eternal law at work in all change. So did Lao Zi, who expressed this idea in terms of *Tao*, the course of things, the principle that governs the development of all things. This fundamental postulate（先决因素） is the "great primal beginning of all that exists", *Taiji*（太极）, in its original meaning the "ridgepole." Later Chinese philosophers devoted much thought to this idea of a primal beginning.

The second element fundamental to *I-Ching* is its theory of ideas. The eight trigrams are images not so much of objects as of states of things. This view is associated with the concept that *every event in the visible world is the effect of an "image,"* that is, of an idea in the unseen world. Accordingly, everything that happens on Earth is only a reproduction of an event in a world beyond our sense perception. This theory of idea is applied in a twofold sense. *I-Ching* not only shows the images of events but also unfolds their conditions in statu nascendi. Thus, in discerning with its help the seeds of things to come, we learn to foresee the future as well as understand the past. In this way, the images on which the hexagrams are based serve as patterns for timely action in the situation indicated.

The third element fundamental to *I-Ching* is the judgements, which, as it were, clothe the images in words. They indicate whether a given action will bring good fortune or bad fortune, remorse or humiliation. The judgements make it possible for a man to make a decision to desist from a course of action indicated by the situation of the moment but harmful in the long run. In its judgement and interpretation, *I-Ching* opens to the reader a richest treasure of Chinese wisdom; at the same time it affords him a comprehensive view of the varieties of human experience, enabling him to shape a life of his own sovereign will into an organic whole and so to direct it into accord with the ultimate *Tao* lying at the root of all that exists.

Book of History（《尚书》）

The *Book of History* is traditionally regarded as "a book of ancient times" (上古之书). "Shang"（尚）in ancient times means "上古." The book records the historical facts of the very ancient period from Yao, Shun, and Yu(尧、舜、禹) down to early Zhou Dynasty.

The traditional account of Chinese history begins with a number of vague, semi-divine cultural heroes who are said to have taught the Chinese people the various arts of civilization. For instance, Pangu(盘古) separates the sky from the earth; Nüwa(女娲) makes men with yellow clay and mends the sky; Shennong(神农) tastes hundreds of wild plants and teaches people to start agriculture. These legendary figures are followed by three rulers of exceptional wisdom and virtue: Yao, Shun and Yu. Yu was the founder of Xia, the first dynasty of Chinese history. This Xia Dynasty, which is supposed to have lasted some three hundred years, was brought to an end when the last ruler Jie(桀), an exceedingly cruel and degenerate king, was overthrown by Tang(汤), who founded the second dynasty, the Shang or Yin. Up to this point, we have no reliable evidence to confirm the existence of any of these men or their reign. For the existence of Shang, however, we have not only archaeological proof but also bone inscriptions that tell about the life of this period. The Shang Dynasty was in turn overthrown by King Wen(文王) and his son King Wu(武王) who set up a new dynasty, the Zhou(周朝) which lasted until 221 B.C.E. and for it and its history we have not only considerable archaeological evidence but also numerous texts of unquestionable authenticity.

The existent texts of the book consist of 58 essays, classified into: *Book of Yu* (《虞书》), 5 essays; *Book of Xia*(《夏书》), 4 essays; *Book of Shang*(《商书》), 17 essays and *Book of Zhou*(《周书》), 32 essays. In terms of literary forms they are divided into ten styles but we can group them into four categories: *Tien*(典), canon or document; *Xunhao*(训诰), instructions and announcements; *Shi*(誓), oath and *Ming*(命), order.

The central theme of the book may be four-fold: respect to the will of Heaven(敬天), exemplification of illustrious virtues(明德), caution in giving punishment(慎罚) and protection of the people(保民). From ancient times this book has been used by emperors and princes, generals and ministers as the principle to achieve peace and order for the state, by workers and businessmen, scholars and common folk as the doctrine to cultivate their personality and deal with their business.

In terms of literary value, this book has opened up a path for the creation of classical essays. Being vividly descriptive and figurative, the essays in the *Book of History* have set a brilliant example and laid down the basis for the creation of essays for later generations.

The *Book of History* has also provided us with important materials for the study of the abstruse and refined language of the Shang and Zhou periods and an important reference in the study of inscriptions on ancient bronzes and stone tablets, on tortoise shells, bones, and ancient utensils.

In short, the *Book of History* is one of the most invaluable documents for the study of Chinese history.

Book of Odes (*Book of Poetry*, *Book of Songs*, *Classic of Poetry* 《诗经》)

The *Book of Odes* is the first collection of poems in the Chinese history, representing the poetry during the five hundred years from the early Western Zhou Dynasty (11th century B.C.E.) to the end of the Spring and Autumn Period (5th century B.C.E.) and, to some extent, reflecting the rise and fall of China's slavery society and the emergence of feudalism.

The book had as its earliest name "Songs" or "300 Songs." It was said to have been edited by Confucius and revered as one of the Confucian classics in the Han Dynasty.

The *Book of Odes* is divided into three parts: *Feng* (Aires), *Ya* (Odes) and *Song* (Eulogies). The origin of this classification can be traced to the categorization of music into *Feng* (tone, hence *Guo Feng, Air from the States*), *Ya* (formal or official music played in court, hence *Da Ya, Great Odes*, which are ancient, and *Xiao Ya, Lesser Odes*, which are new), and *Song* (music for celebration of sacrifice rituals).

Most of the works in the book are folk songs compiled over a period of more than 500 years from different regions of the country. The songs could have been edited by the court musicians or others when matched with music. Besides folk songs, the *Book of Odes* records some works from the upper-class society. Professional officials such as wizards and historians might have authored the songs for sacrifice, banquets, expeditions and hunting.

In the *Book of Odes*, works made in the early years of the Western Zhou Dynasty are now considered valuable reference to the Zhou society. For instance, the song *Qi Yue* (*The Seventh Month*) describes the toil of the poor people all the year round. *Da Ya: Sang Rou* depicts the people's sufferings from the endless turmoil in the late years of the Western Zhou Dynasty. Some other songs, such as *Suo Shu* (*Big Rats*) eulogizes the people at work and accuses the ruling class who, like big rats, gained without pains. The *Book of Odes* also includes poems of love, such as the graceful *Guo Feng: Guan Ju* that tells of a boy's falling in love with a beautiful girl collecting mallows by the river.

In the *Book of Odes*, the language is vivid and vigorous, touching and easy to understand. Double-tone words, rhyme, word overlapping and different patterns of rhymes are used. The verses normally have four-word lines. But there are also cases of 3, 5, 6 or more. Stanza repetitions are quite common.

In many ways, the *Book of Odes* reflects the reality of the society. This tradition of realism had exerted a deep and far-reaching influence on the folk songs and poems in the Han, Wei, Tang and Song Dynasties. Its terse, vivid language and refined artistic style have been objects of imitation in later generations and the book still enjoys a wide readership today.

Book of Rites（《礼记》）

The *Book of Rites*, or the *Book of Rites of Little Dai*, is one of the "Five Classics" of Confucianism and also one of the Thirteen Classics. But it took a long time to become one of the "Five Classics."

In the beginning, Zhuang Zi defined six classics in his book *Zhuang Zi: The Fate*. They were the *Book of Odes*, the *Book of History*, the *Book of Rites*, the *Music*, the *Book of Change*, and the *Spring and Autumn Annals*. However, it remains unknown whether today's the *Book of Rites* is the one mentioned in Zhuang Zi's book. In the Western Han Dynasty (206 B.C.E.—24 A.D.), the *Book of Rites* was only one of the seventeen chapters in the *Manners and Rites*. And the *Book of Rites* was just the note of "the *Rites*." The former was an appendix that explained and illustrated the latter. It was in the Eastern Han Dynasty that the *Book of Rites* was made independent by Zheng Xuan, a scholar who made explanation for it, thus making it more and more important in the history of Chinese culture. By the Tang Dynasty, the *Book of Rites* had become as important as the *Rites of Zhou*, ranking among the "nine classics." In the Ming Dynasty, the *Book of Rites* took the place of the *Manners and Rites*.

There are 49 chapters in the *Book of Rites*. The book covers the canons, institutions, social customs as well as wedding and funeral rites before the Qin Dynasty, as well as the Confucians' conception of political system, of standard for moral character and of manners for social life. The study of this book helps us understand Confucianism in the pre-Qin times.

What are rites? Rites are, according to the book, what are used to build up proper human relationship, to clarify doubts of any affairs, to explain similarities and differences of things, and to determine what is right and what is wrong. What are rites for then? Without rites, the book says, there would not be any virtue and morality. Without rites, instruction and administration would not be perfect, controversies and lawsuit cannot be judged, status of people in family or of monarch and his subjects cannot be determined. To execute rules and regulations, a government needs rites; to make example for study and work, for waiting upon teachers and masters, rites give standard.

the *Book of Rites* covers a wide range of subject matters. Besides detailing social manners, it teaches people the standards of moral cultivation. Some of the standards are still believed and followed by Chinese people today. For instance, to deal with others, one should "learn from others' strong points to offset his own weakness;" to be with friends, one should "pay a man back in his own coin;" one should "respect the old and love the young." The principles of rites help perfect one's soul and this will show one as respectful and elegant with gentle and cultivated manner. The Chinese nation has a long history of traditional moral education. Thanks to the *Book of Rites*, younger generations can learn and behave well. However, there are still some dross and some over-elaborate formalities, some of which are still seen today and should be abandoned. For instance, women's clothes are not supposed to hang close to men's; the younger are supposed to follow every single word of the elder, no matter it is correct or not.

Spring and Autumn Annals（《春秋》）

A historical record of the state of Lu（鲁）, the *Spring and Autumn Annals* is the first chronicle in China.

The *Spring and Autumn Annals* records Confucius as the claimed writer. Many scholars in the Warring States Period and the Han Dynasty made a similar claim. As a matter of fact, Confucius was not the writer but the editor. The *Spring and Autumn Annals*, written chronologically, records the history of Lu and other states during the period between 772 B.C.E. and 481 B.C.E. The significance of the *Spring and Autumn Annals* lies in the fact that they are a true record of history and the first complete and accurate chronicle in China. Since the Han Dynasty, the *Spring and Autumn Annals* have been revered as one of the Confucian classics and some even claim that "the *Spring and Autumn Annals* is the best record of history." But the *Spring and Autumn Annals* notes down very simple historical facts, with many omissions. This is made worse by the use of implicit diction. Hence, some scholars have prepared explanatory notes and annotations which are called *Zhuan*（"传"）, or commentaries. These include *Gongyang Zhuan*（《公羊传》）, *Guliang Zhuan*（《谷梁传》）, *Zoushi Zhuan*（《邹氏传》）, *Jiashi Zhuan*（《夹氏传》）and others.

Gongyang Zhuan and *Guliang Zhuan* explain the *Spring and Autumn Annals* word by word. The later only explains the literal meanings of the words while the former goes behind the lines to explore the implications.

· *Seminar* ·

What is the philosophy underlying the book *I-Ching*?

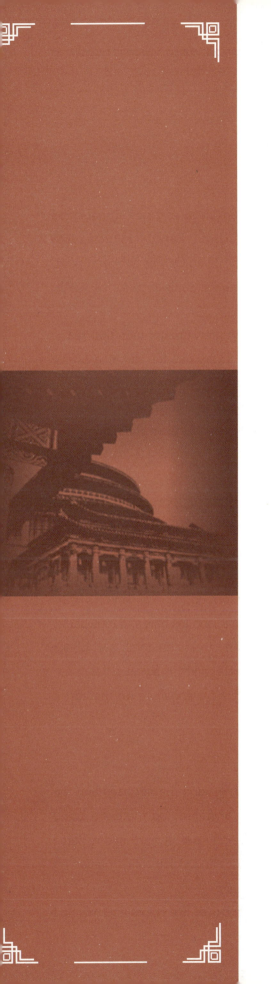

Chapter Three
Literature and Art

- Chinese Myths
- A Summary of Chinese Literature
- Six Arts and Four Treasures of the Studio in Ancient China
- Calligraphy and Painting
- Acrobatic Art, Martial Arts, *Taiji Quan* and *Qigong*
- Beijing Opera and Other Local Operas

I
Chinese Myths

How Pangu Separates the Sky from the Earth（盘古开天地）

In the remote ancient times the universe was a big black mass of gases in the shape of an egg. Pangu was born in it. Eighteen thousand years passed. Pangu had grown into a giant. With a huge axe, he spilt the "Big Egg" in half. The *Yang Qi* was light and pure, rose to become the sky, and the *Yin Qi* was heavy and murky, sank to form the earth. Pangu was between them.

Pangu changed his forms nine times a day. His wisdom grew greater than that of the sky and his ability increased bigger than that of the earth. Every day the sky rose twelve feet higher and the earth became twelve feet thicker, Pangu did the same with them.

Another eighteen thousand years passed. The sky became extremely high and the earth extremely thick. And Pangu also grew extremely tall. His feet were standing on the earth and his head supporting the sky.

Pangu Turns into Everything on Heaven and Earth（盘古化生万物）

After separating the sky from the earth, Pangu changed his forms every day. When he died, his breath became winds and clouds, his voice thunder, his left eye became the sun and his right eye the moon; his arms and legs turned into the four poles of the earth, and the five parts of his body the five mountains; his blood formed the rivers and his veins the roads; his flesh and skin changed into the soil of the fields, and his hair and moustache the stars; the hair on his skin transformed into grasses and trees, his teeth and bones metals and rocks; his marrow changed into pearls and jades, and his sweat fell as rain; the insect on his body was blown by the winds and scattered everywhere on the earth, becoming beasts.

Nüwa Mends the Sky（女娲补天）

In ancient times, the four corners of the sky collapsed, making the sky tilted and the earth split open. The sky could not shelter all the things anymore and the earth could not shoulder all the things on it. A great fire spread violently everywhere and a fierce flood devoured everything on its path. Savage beasts ran riot and vicious birds preyed on people and the other weak animals.

Then Nüwa came out to save the world. She melted rocks of five colors and mended the cracks of the sky with them. She cut off the four legs of the giant turtle and used them to support the four corners of the sky. She killed the black dragon to save people from its flames and blocked the flood with ashes of reeds.

Thus the sky was mended, its four corners lifted up, the flood tamed, and the nine regions returned to peace, the harmful birds and beasts vanished. All the people live happily under the dome of the sky.

Nüwa Makes Men (女娲造人)

When the sky and the earth were separated, there were no men on the earth. Then, Nüwa, a divine figure, made men with yellow clay. The work was so great that Nüwa couldn't finish it with her two hands. She thought of a way for the job — to plunge a rope into the mud and then raise the mud up. The mud that fell from the rope also became men. Those made of moulding yellow clay were rich and noble, while those made by drawing the rope poor and low.

Jingwei Determines to Fill up the Sea (精卫填海)

On the Fajiu Mountain, there was a mulberry forest. In the forest lived a bird named Jingwei. The bird had a black-and-white head, a grey bill and two red claws. It kept calling "Jingwei! Jingwei!"

As the legend has it, Jingwei was the youngest daughter of Emperor Yan, originally named Nüwa (女娃). She was fond of swimming. One day when she was swimming in the East Sea, she was drowned deep in the sea. Her soul, not willing to give in, broke through the water and became a bird. As the calling of the bird is "Jingwei, jingwei," people named it according to its call.

Unable to forget its hatred to the sea, ever day, the bird kept picking up twigs and small stones from the Western Mountain to drop them into the sea. She was determined to avenge herself by filling up the sea!

Nowadays people can still hear the calling "Jingwei! Jingwei!" and see the bird flying back and forth between the Western Mountain and the East Sea, busying herself with her great work — to fill up the sea.

Kuafu Runs a Race with the Sun (夸父追日)

In very, very ancient time, Kuafu, a divine figure, had a race with the sun. When he came too close to the sun, he became burning thirsty. So he drank from the Yellow River and the Wei River. But the waters of the two rivers could not quench his thirst. He turned north, intending to drink from the Great Lake, but he died of thirst on his half way. The walking stick he threw away became a forest of peach trees, giving shelter to the later generations.

The Cow Boy and the Weaving Girl (牛郎和织女)

It is a beautiful legend popular among the Chinese people. On the eastern bank of the Heavenly River lived a weaving girl. She was the daughter of Heavenly Emperor. She worked hard day and night to weave the colorful cloth for gods and goddesses.

To cite her distinguished work, the Heavenly Emperor allowed her to marry the cow boy on the western bank of the river. However, after the marriage, she was indulged in her marriage life and neglected her work. The Heavenly Emperor was so angry that he separated the young couple on each side of the river, and only allowed them to meet once a year on the 7th day of lunar year.

On that day magpies would gather together to form a bridge across the river for the young lovers to pass. The down on the heads of the birds were worn out for the work. That's why magpies would suddenly become bald-headed on the day of July 7 each year.

Chang'e Flies to the Moon (嫦娥奔月)

As the legend has it, in ancient times, there appeared ten suns in the sky, baking people and plants on the earth. Houyi (后羿) shot down nine of them, letting one remain to give people warmth and light. As a reward, the Queen of the West gave him a pill of immortality. His wife, Chang'e stole and ate the pill. Then she flied to the moon and turned into a toad, which is called the Spirit of the Moon.

As another legend goes, there was a laurel tree and a toad on the moon. The tree was five thousand feet tall. Under it there was a man chopping at it all the time. However, the tree healed itself after each wound. The man was called Wugang (吴刚) from Xihe. He committed some errors in learning to become an immortal and was fined to chop the tree on the moon.

II
A Summary of Chinese Literature

Classical Literature (古典文学)

Classical Chinese literature refers to the period from the days before the Qin Dynasty

(221 B.C.E.—207 B.C.E.) to the Opium War of 1840 during the Qing Dynasty (1644 A.D.—1911 A.D.). It is traditionally sub-divided into the following periods:

Pre—Qin Literature (先秦文学)

In this period four books are worth mentioning:

Book of Songs or Book of Odes (《诗经》)

The book was composed during the Western Zhou Dynasty (1100 B.C.E.—770 B.C.E.) and the Spring and Autumn Period (770 B.C.E.—476 B.C.E.), marking the beginning of China's 3,000 years of literary history. Edited by Confucius, it is an anthology of about three hundred poems. Some of them are folk songs from the feudal states of early Zhou times while others are songs used by the nobles in sacrificial ceremonies or at banquets.

Li Sao or The Lament (《离骚》)

The book was written during the Warring States Period (475 B.C.E.—221 B.C.E.) by the great patriotic poet Qu Yuan (屈原, 340 B.C.E.—278 B.C.E.) who is regarded as "father of Chinese poetry," carrying Chinese literature to its first peak.

Li Sao, consisting of 373 lines and 2,490 characters, is the longest and greatest lyric in ancient China. Lyrical and romantic, the poem portrays a most brilliant figure— Qu Yuan himself, successfully conveying his life and struggle, thoughts and feelings through the alternative application of vivid narration.

Book of the Mountains and Seas (《山海经》)

Book of the Mountains and Seas is a unique encyclopedia generally believed to be collectively compiled before the Qin Dynasty.

Its contents, centering around geography, cover many other disciplines, such as, zoology, botany, mineralogy, phenology, meteorology, astronomy, agronomy, animal husbandry, hydraulic engineering, handicraft, transportation, armament, architecture, textile processing, medical science, pharmaceutics, nutriology, genesiology, mathematics, geodesy, astronautics, systematics, anthropology, ethnonymics, sociology, history, folklore, literature and art, politics, military, ethics, religion, mythology, aesthetics, and philosophy.

It is interesting to note that there were pictures originally attached to the book.

Analects (《论语》)

Analects is the most important work of the Confucian literary heritage. Compiled by Confucius's disciples, it is a record of the master's activities and conversations, the only reliable source about the life and teachings of this great teacher. The book contains 20 chapters and 497 verses, some consisting of the briefest maxims. From the time when Confucianism became widely accepted, the laconic and provocative sentences of this work have exercised a profound impact upon the thought and language of the Chinese intellectuals. For the last eight hundred years it has become a basic text in Chinese education known to every schoolboy.

Literature of the Qin and Han Dynasties（秦汉文学，221 B.C.E.—220 A.D.）

In this period we should draw your attention to the following two works:

Historical Records by Sima Qian （司马迁：《史记》）

As we have mentioned before, it is a model of prose writing which was studied and inherited by writers of the Song and Tang Dynasties.

Flight of the Phoenix to the Southeast （《孔雀东南飞》）

In the Han Dynasty there appeared a new kind of poetry called *Yuefu*（乐府）. Originally it was an official constitution for collecting folk songs and composing music for them. Later it became the general term for the folk songs collected. According to the *Book of Han*（《汉书》） there were 138 folk songs of Han *Yuefu*, with only 40 still existent.

Yuefu is another peak of Chinese classical poetry after *Book of Odes*（《诗经》） and *Chuci*（《楚辞》—Qu Yuan's poems）, among them the most famous is a long narrative poem *Flight of the Phoenix to the Southeast*, also translated as *As Evergreen As the Fir*, telling about the tragic story of a young girl.

Literature of the Wei, Jin, Southern and Northern Dynasties（魏晋南北朝文学，220 A.D.—581 A.D.）

Poetry flourished in the Wei and Jin dynasties（220 A.D.—420 A.D.）, marking another peak in the history of Chinese literature. Cao Cao（曹操，155 A.D.—220 A.D.）, Cao Zhi（曹植，192 A.D.—232 A.D.）, Ruan Ji（阮籍，210 A.D.—263 A.D.） and Ji Kang（嵇康，223 A.D.—262 A.D.） were outstanding men of letters of this time and Tao Yuanming（陶渊明，365 or 372 A.D.—427 A.D.）was particularly noted for his idyllic poems. The Southern and Northern Dynasties（420 A.D.—581 A.D.） were known for their folk songs. Love songs predominated in the Southern Dynasties whereas folk songs expressing people's militancy were a prominent feature of the Northern Dynasties. *The Song of Mulan*（《木兰辞》） is the best-known among the latter type.

An Anthology of Cao Cao（《曹操集》）

The anthology is a collection of more than 20 poems by Cao Cao who was the founder of the Jian'an literature and the Jian'an style（建安文学和建安风骨）.

In Cao Cao's poems, heroism and great ease dominate the theme throughout his life. Even in his old age, when he sighed at the impermanence of life, his works were brimming with an optimistic and enterprising spirit. Take a sentence for example, "An old steed in the stable still longs to gallop a thousand *li*; a senior person of high endeavor never abandons his aspiration."（老骥伏枥，志在千里；烈士暮年，壮心不已。）These sentences are still catchwords among the people even today.

Collected Works of Tao Yuanming（《陶渊明集》）

The book contains poems and prose writings by Tao Yuanming, a master of the *Yinyi* School of Poetry（隐逸派）. Disillusioned by the darkness of society and the ups and downs in politics, he retired from his government post and chose to live in seclusion. Most of his poems are idyllic lyrics written in his days of seclusion, with *Return to Rural Life*（《归去来辞》）, *House-moving*（《移居》）, *Memory of the Rural Cottage*（《怀古田舍》）being the most famous. The lyrics described the rural scenery, the poet's engagement in farm work to support himself, and the straits of his life as a hermit.

His well-known prose masterpiece *The Peach Garden*（《桃花源记》）paints a vivid picture of a fictitious land where the people are well-clad and well-fed.

Stories of Immortals（《搜神记》）

There was a boom of mythical stories in the Han, Wei and Six Dynasties due to the popularity of various schools of religious thought. Mythical stories in this period kept accounts of large numbers of ancient myths, legends, fantastic stories and anecdotes. Rich and vivid in content, complicated and fantastic in plot, they are of high artistic value and are part of the splendid Chinese cultural heritage.

Stories of Immortals, also translated as *Notes of Collecting Gods* or *Records of Spirits*, is a collection of the mythical stories of those days. A mixture of Confucianism, alchemy, witchcraft and the superstitious sect of Taoism, the book preserves remarkable folktales and tales of marvels, their contents embracing the criticism of the cruel and ferocious ruling class and the praise of the oppressed working people, the description of the miseries and hardships of the laboring masses, as well as the struggle of the young for the freedom of love. Also, among them are myths and ghost stories.

The Joke Forest（《笑林》）

Compiled by Handan Chun（邯郸淳）, *The Joke Forest* (also translated as *Xiao Lin* or *Jest Books*) is China's first collection of jokes.

Most of the jokes collected in *The Joke Forest* are satirical in nature, targeting rich misers, cunning villains, toadies and plagiarists. It also contains fables, providing the readers with a moral lesson while making them laugh.

As the first collection of jokes in ancient China, *The Joke Forest* was to have great influence upon the writing of both jokes and fables in later generations.

Literary Mind and Carving of Dragons（*Carving a Dragon at the Core of Literature*）（《文心雕龙》）

Literary Mind and Carving of Dragons, China's first book on literary criticism, was written by Liu Xie（刘勰）, styled Yanhe（字彦和）, a literary theorist and critic of the Southern Dynasties.

Literary Mind and Carving of Dragons is a fifty-chapter treatise on literary principles and criticism. It's contents are introduced in *Author's Will*（《序志》）, the last chapter of the book. The first 5 chapters, from *Pursuing the Way*（《原道》）to *Defense of Li Sao*（《辨骚》）, are the pivot of the whole book, showing the author's basic view on literature. The next 20 chapters, from *On Poetry*（《明诗》）to *Letters and Memorials*（《书记》）, are the study of stylistics and the individual literary history, systematically discussing the nature, development and key writing points of literary works of various styles. The following 19 chapters, from *Imagination*（《神思》）to *General Principle*（《总述》）, together with *Emotions and Outlooks*（《物色》）, are the principles of creative writing, ranging from general guidelines to specific techniques. *Age and Literature*（《时序》）and *Writer's Acumen*（《才略》） are two chapters on writers and the history of literature, briefly evaluating the renowned writers and their works through the ages. *Perception and Appreciatio*（《知音》）and *Writer's Moral Character*（《程器》）deal with the key issues in literary criticism.

The purpose of Liu Xie in writing this book is to criticize the efforts of his contemporaries to seek the beauty in form at the cost of the Meaning and advocate the presence of social and political content in literature. Liu Xie holds that form and content should go hand in hand, giving superiority of the meaning over the form. *Literary Mind and Carving of Dragons* sums up the literary trends in the previous times and ushers in a new era of literary theory and criticism.

Literature of the Tang Dynasty（唐代文学, 618 A.D.—907 A.D.）

The Tang Dynasty was both economically and culturally an age of unprecedented prosperity. Its literature, especially poetry, reached a zenith in history. *The Complete Collection of Tang Poems*（《全唐诗》）, edited in the early Qing Dynasty, comprises 48,977 poems by 2,208 poets, of which the most well-known are Li Bai（李白, 701 A.D.—762 A.D.）, Du Fu（杜甫, 712 A.D.—770 A.D.）and Bai Juyi（白居易, 772 A.D.—846 A.D.）.

An Anthology of Li Taibai（《李太白诗集》）

Li Bai, styled Taibai, is the greatest romantic poet in ancient China after Qu Yuan. He carried forward the fine literary tradition of romanticism in early Chinese poetry represented by *Chuci* and *Yuefu*. His poems, vigorous and enthusiastic, permeated with active romanticism, are lucid, lively and stirring, reaching the pinnacle of classical poetry.

The book *An Anthology of Li Taibai* contains about 1,000 poems, covering a wide range of subjects, from the exposition of corruption of the court and the hard life and sufferings of the people, to the description of magnificent scenery of the country as well as the eulogy of true friendship and the expression of his ideals and feelings.

Let's quote one of his poems to show his lyrical and innovative imagery and his beauty of language.

朝辞白帝彩云间, 千里江陵一日还。

两岸猿声啼不住, 轻舟已过万重山。

Leaving at dawn the White Emperor crowned with cloud,

I've sailed a thousand *li* through Canyon in a day.

With the monkey's adieus the riverbanks are loud,

my skiff has left ten thousand mountains far away.

（Translated by Xu Yuanchong）

An Anthology of Du Fu（《杜工部诗集》）

Du Fu was the greatest poet of realism in ancient China. A mirror of the times, his poems faithfully and profoundly reflect the social realities of the Tang Dynasty in decline, like a historical account written in poetry. Thus they have been called "history in poems."

In 759 A.D. he gave up his official post and went to Sichuan Province, making his abode in a thatched hut on the outskirts of Chengdu. For a time, he worked for the local commissioner Yan Wu（剑南节度史严武）as Gongbu Yuanwailang（工部员外郎）, a minor official in the Board of Works. So his contemporaries called him Du Gongbu（杜工部）.

More than 1, 400 of his poems are retained to the present day, covering various aspects of the society of his time. Many of them are penetrating exposures of the iniquities of the ruling class and the sufferings of the people. Following are his most famous lines:

Wine and meat stink behind vermilion gates, while at the roadside, people freeze to death. （朱门酒肉臭，路有冻死骨。）

An Anthology of Bai Xiangshan（《白香山诗集》）

Bai Juyi is another influential Tang poet whose works are characterized by vivid image, plain language and profound sympathy for the common people. In his later years, he showed great interest in Buddhism and often stayed in the Xiangshan Temple in LuoYang（洛阳香山寺）, hence he got his sobriquet of "Lay Buddhist in Xiangshan"（香山居士） and his popular name of "Bai Xiangshan." More than three thousands of his poems have passed down to us, surpassing all other Tang poets in quantity. Among them the most well-known are *The Old Man Selling Charcoal*（《卖炭翁》）, *Song of Eternal Sorrow* （《长恨歌》）and *Song of a Pipa Girl*（《琵琶行》）. The first depicts the tragic story of an old man, in which the couplet is well-known: "Though his coat is thin he hopes for winter, for cold weather will keep up the price of fuel."（可怜身上衣正单，心忧炭贱愿天寒。） The second is based on a legend of the love story between Emperor Tang Minghuang（唐明皇） and his favorite concubine Yang Guifei（杨贵妃）. With a strong element of lyric atmosphere, *Song of Eternal Sorrow* is considered a fine work in which realism mingles well with romanticism. The third expressed his lament over his own destiny by narrating the unfortunate life of a skillful pipa girl. Both excellent in content and language, *Song of the Pipa Girl* ranks a masterpiece, appealling to people across the centuries.

Literature of the Song Dynasty（宋代文学，960 A.D.—1279 A.D.）

The Song Dynasty literature is renowned for its *Ci*（词）poems（*Ci*, a form of poetry consisting of lines of different lengths）. In its early period, *Ci* described mainly the sentiments and parting sorrow between a gentleman and his beloved. The main representatives of this school of *Ci* writers were Liu Yong（柳永，1004 A.D.—1054 A.D）, Zhou Bangyan（周邦彦，1057 A.D—1121 A.D）and Li Qingzhao（李清照，1084 A.D—1151 A.D）. Towards the end of the Northern Song Dynasty appeared Su Shi（苏轼，1036 A.D—1101 A.D）and Xin Qiji（辛弃疾，1140 A.D—1027 A.D）. The former used *Ci* to describe natural scenes and expressed his emotions while the latter filled his poems with grief and indignation. The Southern Song Dynasty produced a host of *Ci* writers of their calibre, the best-known being

Yue Fei(岳飞, 1103 A.D—1042 A.D) and Wen Tianxiang (文天祥, 1236 A.D—1282 A.D).

The Song Dynasty also had many famous writers of prose and poetry, Wang Anshi(王安石, 1021 A.D—1086 A.D)and Su Shi of the Northern Song period and Lu You(陆游, 1125 A.D—1210 A.D)of the Southern Song being the most outstanding. Su Shi(苏轼), Su Xun(苏洵, 1009 A.D—1066 A.D), Su Zhe(苏辙, 1039 A.D—1112 A.D), Ouyang Xiu(欧阳修, 1007 A.D—1072 A.D), Wang Anshi and Zeng Gong(曾巩, 1019 A.D—1083 A.D), together with Tang writers Han Yu(韩愈, 768 A.D—824 A.D)and Liu Zongyuan(柳宗元, 772 A.D—846 A.D)are called "eight great essayists of the Tang and Song Dynasties"(唐宋八大家). Their writings, both lucid and smooth in style, had a profound effect on later prose writing.

A Collection of Li Qingzhao's Works(《李清照集》)

This collection includes the works of Li Qingzhao, the first outstanding female *Ci* poet in China.

Li Qingzhao's works are strong and sincere in emotion, plain, fresh, graceful as well as restrained in style. She is good at expressing her joy and sorrow in simple but profound words and in a gentle and fluent tone. Her smiles and tears can be easily discerned in her plain and rhythmical diction. Only the emperor-poet Li Yu(李煜)could rival her in lyric *Ci* poetry. Let's quote her *Spring Morning*(《如梦令·春晓》) for example:

昨夜雨疏风骤，浓睡不消残酒。

试问卷帘人，却道海棠依旧。

知否? 知否? 应是绿肥红瘦。

Last night the rain was scattered,

The gust strong,

Deep slumber did not ease my hangover long.

I querried the one rolling up the blinds,

And was told the flowering crabapples have kept their prime.

Do you not know?

Do you not know?

Now is the time when green should be corpulent

And red should be gaunt.

(Translated by Gong Jinghao)

The Collected Works of Lu You(《陆游集》)

The Collected Works of Lu You contains 9,300 poems by Lu You, an outstanding patriotic poet in the Southern Song Dynasty. Among his poems, those that express the poet's love for the country are far more outstanding. His poems not only reflect the wishes of the people for a united country but also criticize the surrender and submissiveness of the rulers. In them, the poet expressed his firm determination to join the army and sacrifice for the country as well as his such unfulfilled ambitions. *The Storm on November 4th*（《十一月四日风雨大作》） reads:

僵卧荒村不自哀，尚思为国戍轮台。

夜阑卧听风吹雨，铁马冰河入梦来。

In desolate village I lie stiff but not sad,

Still thinking about defending the nation instead.

The rain soaks the wind that blows the dead of the night,

And armored horses and frozen rivers enter my dream meanwhile.

Lu You longed for the unification of the country even before he died at 85, when he left a swan song *To Show to My Son*（《示儿诗》）:

死去原知万事空，但悲不见九洲同。

王师北定中原日，家祭无忘告乃翁。

Dying, I know all things are empty,

Still I grieve I never saw the Nine Provinces united.

The day the King's armies march north to take the heartland,

At the family sacrifice don't forget to let your father know.

The Collected Works of Su Dongpo（《苏东坡集》）

Written by Su Shi in the Song Dynasty, *The Collected Works of Su Dongpo* is a collection of masterpieces of poems, *Ci* poems and prose.

Su Shi, styled Zizhan（子瞻）, also known as "the Lay Buddhist Monk Dougpo"（东坡居士）, was born into a poor intellectual family in Meishan（眉山，now in Sichuan Province）. Su Shi, as well as his father Su Xun（苏洵）and his younger brother Su Zhe（苏辙）, were well-known men of letters in the Northern Song Dynasty.

Su Shi developed a style of prose that was marked by ease and simplicity. Free from restriction of forms, his prose writing touches upon a wide range of themes and employs flexible techniques of expression. His writings are as free as "floating clouds and running water, without a fixed nature, going where proper and stopping where they should."（如

行云流水，初无定质，但常行于所当行，常止于不可不止。）

Su Shi's poems share the same style with his prose, which is varied in themes and written in a vigorous and fluent style, brimming with talent and wisdom.

Su Shi's *Ci* poems emerged as a thunderbolt in the literary circle of his time. He widened the realm, freed the form and bettered the artistic conception of *Ci* poetry. His *Niannujiao: Memories of Chibi*（《念奴娇·赤壁怀古》）, honored as a swan song of *Ci* poems through the ages, recounts the spectacular scene of the ancient battle field and portrays a shining image of the ancient hero Zhou Yu（周瑜）.

Literature of the Yuan Dynasty（元代文学，1271 A.D.—1368 A.D.）

Zaju（杂剧） or drama, was the greatest achievement in the literature of the Yuan Dynasty, and had a far-reaching influence on the later development of play-writing and acting as well as on the rise of various forms of operas. Three hundred and forty-five *Zaju* plays have been handed down to us, 63 of which were written by the well-known playwright Guan Hanqing（关汉卿，1229 A.D.—1297 A.D.）. His *Snow in Midsummer*（《窦娥冤》） and Wang Shifu's（王实甫，1260 A.D.—1336 A.D.） *The West Chamber*（《西厢记》） are masterpieces widely read over the centuries.

It is interesting to note that Guan Hanqing and Shakespeare（1564 A.D.—1616 A.D.） lived almost in the same period of history（to be exact, Guan is three hundred years before Shakespeare）, Shakespeare had written 37 plays while our Guan Hanqing had 63.

Collected Works of Guan Hanqing（《关汉卿戏曲集》）

Collected Works of Guan Hanqing includes all the plays written by Guan Hanqing in the Yuan Dynasty. Guan's works lay the foundation for Chinese drama.

The Yuan Dynasty ushered in a golden age of Chinese drama. Among numerous playwrights of the time, Guan Hanqing was definitely the most outstanding representative and the greatest figure in the history of Chinese drama.

During his lifetime, Guan Hanqing wrote more than sixty types of *Zaju*, or Chinese poetic drama set to music. Most of the plays convey the writer's indignation and hatred for the oppressors and his deep sympathy for the oppressed, eulogizing the indomitable and resourceful struggle of the oppressed.

Guan's drama represents a variety of artistic styles. There are tragedies that open up a unique road for Chinese tragedy writing. Filled with grief and indignation, the tragedies usually end with the failure of the evil force and the victory of the good, satisfying and touching readers to the heart. Among them *Snow in Midsummer* or *Injustice of Dou E* is a model for Chinese playwrights and one of the greatest tragedies in the world. There are comedies, some being serious as *Saving Women*（《救风尘》） while others as light as *The Riverside Pavilion*（《望江亭》）. There are also historical plays, which are full of heroism and encouragement.

Guan Hanqing was a master playwright of his time, whose influence benefited generations to come. Over the past centuries, his plays have remained important programs on the stage.

Romance of the Western Chamber（《西厢记》）

Written by Wang Shifu, *Romance of the Western Chamber* is the best ancient love play in China. It eulogizes the true love between Cui YingYing（崔莺莺） and Zhang Sheng （张生）.

Pursuing the ideal that "all lovers under the heaven should be united"（有情人终成眷属）, the playwright fights against the feudal marriage system and sets out to reveal the deep-rooted conflicts in China's feudal society. Therefore, the play reaches an unprecedented ideological height of love stories.

Romance of the Western Chamber is characterized by outstanding artistic achievements. In characterization, the play reveals the delicate and complicated inner activities of the characters in a meticulous and subtle way so as to figure out their personality traits. Besides, the play displays the characters by interweaving truth with fiction and by employing light and shade. The play is grand and compact in structure, opens and closes in the right places. Linguistically, it's resplendent, natural and rich in temperament and interest.

Jin Shengtan（金圣叹）, a famous critic in the Qing Dynasty, put *Romance of the Western Chamber* among *Li Sao*, *Zhuang Zi*, *Historical Records*, *Du Fu*, and *Outlaws of the Marsh*, calling them "Book of masters."

Literature of the Ming and Qing Dynasties（明清文学, 1368 A.D.—1840 A.D.）

The Ming and Qing Dynasties were a great period of fiction and drama. Famous plays of the Ming Dynasty include *The Tale of the Lute*（《琵琶记》） by Gao Ming（高明, 1305 A.D.—1380 A.D.） and *The Peony Pavilion*（《牡丹亭》） by Tang Xianzu（汤显祖, 1550 A.D.—1617 A.D.）; the best Qing plays are *The Peach-Blossom Fan*（《桃花扇》） by Kong Shangren（孔尚任, 1648 A.D.—1718 A.D.） and *The Palace of Eternal Youth* （《长生殿》）by Hong Sheng（洪昇, 1645 A.D.—1704 A.D.）. Especially note-worthy are the full-length novels which evolved from the story-tellers' scripts of the Song and Yuan Dynasties. The appearance of the four great novels of the Ming Dynasty *Outlaws of the*

Marsh（《水浒传》） by Shi Naian（施耐庵,1296 A.D.—1370 A.D.）, *Romance of the Three Kingdoms*（《三国演义》） by Luo Guanzhong（罗贯中, 1330 A.D.—1400 A.D.）, *Journey to the West*（《西游记》）by Wu Chengen（吴承恩, 1500 A.D.—1582 A.D.） and *Jin Ping Mei*（《金瓶梅》） by Lan Ling Xiao Xiaosheng（兰陵笑笑生） shows that novel-writing had reached maturity. The Qing Dynasty featured with such works as *The Scholars* （《儒林外史》）, a satirical novel by Wu Jingzi（吴敬梓, 1701 A.D.—1754 A.D.） and Cao Xueqin's（曹雪芹, 1719 A.D.—1763 A.D.） masterpiece, *A Dream of Red Mansions*（《红楼梦》）. Pu Songling's（蒲松龄, 1640 A.D.—1715 A.D.） collection of short stories, *Strange Tales from the Carefree Studio*（《聊斋志异》）, is also a famous work of the Qing period. It takes its material from stories about ghosts and fox spirits. Through these tales, the author censures the evils of the society in which he lived.

Outlaws of the Marsh（《水浒传》）

Outlaws of the Marsh, also translated as *Water Margin, Heroes of the Marsh, All Men Are Brothers*, tells of 108 outlaws under the green wood headed by Song Jiang（宋江）. The story takes place in Liangshan in a peasants' revolt during the reign of Emperor Huizong （宋徽宗） of the Song Dynasty. The greenwood men were of different social backgrounds: petty officials, low-rank officers, peasants, the urban poor, peddlers, as well as Buddhist and Taoist monks. The dark rule of the Song Dynasty had forced them up the Liangshan Mountain and Shuipo Marsh under the banner of brotherhood. The Liangshan band began with only a few dozens of men and gradually grew into an army of thousands. Under the slogan of "Enforcing justice on behalf of Heaven, safeguarding the land and protecting the people"（替天行道, 保境安民）, they challenged the forces of the court and killed local despots. Having seen its glorious days, this peasant army finally accepted amnesty and surrender. Later on, it was sent to fight the army of another peasants' uprising and Song Jiang came to the end of his row.

The author creates over 108 figures in the novel by showing their different features, clothes, gestures, voices, countenances and motions with their distinct character. For example, the name of Lu Zhishen（鲁智深） reminds us of a Buddhist monk with a round face, big ears, dense whiskers, and a thunderous voice, always carrying a staff（禅杖）. So does the name of Li Kui（李逵） who has a ferocious character and yellow hair, eating big pieces of meat and drinking big bowls of wine. The name of Song Jiang（宋江） comes to one's mind as a short, witty and silent man with a blackened face. The language in the fiction is characterized by vividness, distinctness and strong folk flavor.

For its ideological and artistic achievements, *Outlaws of the Marsh* is now regarded as a great epic of the peasants' wars in feudal China.

The Romance of the Three Kingdoms（《三国演义》）

The Romance of the Three Kingdoms, a 120-chapter historical novel, one of the four literary masterpieces in the Ming Dynasty, has for centuries been a most welcomed reader among the people. The subject of the novel draws from the history between the last years of the Eastern Han Dynasty and the Three Kingdoms of Wei, Shu and Wu, covering almost one century. The novel incorporates a large number of characters and a series of complicated events into this legendary century of history. Special emphasis is laid on Liu Bei（刘备） and Cao Cao（曹操）, two antagonistic figures in the ruling class. Liu Bei is portrayed as an ideal ruler, who carries out the Kingly Way（王道）and Benevolent Politics（仁政）. His antagonist Cao Cao, however, was in history a famous statesman, strategist and poet, and he played a considerable part in unifying Northern China in the chaotic period of the three kingdoms. Besides, Zhuge Liang（诸葛亮）, Guo Jia（郭嘉）, Guan Yu（关羽）, Sun Quan（孙权）, Xiahou Dun（夏侯敦）, Huang Gai（黄盖）, Lü Meng（吕蒙）, Zhang Fei（张飞）, Zhao Yun（赵云）and Huang Zhong（黄忠） are also distinct characters and artistic images. Zhuge Liang is depicted as an outstanding statesman and a strategist whose foresight is godlike.

Taking the conflicts and struggles as a major clue and wars as plots, the writer strings hundreds of tales together with distinct cause and effect, and combines facts with imagination, details with sketches, interposed narration with flashback, creating a masterpiece that is surpassed by few in Chinese history.

Journey to the West（《西游记》）

Unlike other ancient Chinese novels, *Journey to the West*（also translated as *The Pilgrimage to the West, Story of a Long Journey to the West, Monkey King*） incorporates both myths and fairy tales. But, similar to *Outlaws of the Marsh* and *Romance of the Three Kingdoms*, the novel is based on folk tales and stories that had long been popular among the people before it was finally compiled and revised by the author.

The novel criticizes the fatuity, incompetence, licentiousness and savagery of the ruling class. Emperors on Earth either believe in Taoism or indulge in women. Even the Jade Emperor（玉帝）, a solemn image in Heaven, is also an arbitrary tyrant who is unable to discriminate between the virtuous and the stupid. The demons and ghosts on their way are apotheoses（神化）for the natural dangers and difficulties; more of them are symbols of evil powers endangering people and society.

Religion is an object of mockery in the novel. Pig Bajie（猪八戒）pokes fun at the three Taoist gods of Luck, Fortune and Longevity（福、禄、寿三星）. Monkey King（孙悟空）jeers at Buddha Rulai（如来佛）to his face and says that he is the nephew of the demon. The rebellious spirit of the hero Monkey King is eulogized through account of his storming the heavenly palace and ravaging the nether regions.

Journey to the West represents a pinnacle in Chinese fiction and it is a rare and excellent mythical work in the literary history of China and the world.

A Dream of Red Mansions（《红楼梦》）

Being one of the four famous Chinese classics, *A Dream of Red Mansions*（also translated as *The Story of the Stone*）was written by Cao Xueqin（曹雪芹） and completed by Gao E（高鹗） in the mid-eighteenth century. It is, to some extent, an autobiography with a high degree of ideological content and artistic quality, in which the author narrates the decline of the four clans of Jia（贾）, Shi（史）, Wang（王） and Xue（薛）, with a key thread of the love between Jia Baoyu（贾宝玉）, Lin Daiyu（林黛玉） and Xue Baochai（薛宝钗）. The hero and two heroines dominate among the 975 characters in the novel, and their tragic love affairs play a central role throughout the 120-chapter story. However, most characters and plots do not have direct link with the theme of love. It is obvious that the writer's pen goes far beyond the scope of love and marriage. More important is the narration of the decline of the feudal families. Every character and every development of plot center on this theme.

In the novel, the writer's criticism targets every facet of the feudal social superstructure, such as the systems of bureaucracy and imperial examinations, the ethics of family and marriage, as well as the use of maidservants and the exploitation of the peasants. He exposes and negates the hypocrisy and irrationality of the feudal morality.

The language of the novel marks a summit in the art of language in Chinese classic stories. The author uses only a couple of words to sketch each of the character who are so vividly created that they leave the readers with deep impressions.

The author's narration boasts a high artistic quality; the verses, ditties, odes and songs（诗词曲赋） not only fuse together with narration, but also help to create typical characteristics. *A Dream of Red Mansions*, with unique characters and eternal artistic charms in both content and form, has its firm place in the world literature.

Modern Literature（现代文学, 1840 A.D.—1919 A.D.）

Literature of the period between the Opium War of 1840 and the May 4th Movement of 1919 is referred to as modern Chinese literature. Works of this period feature themselves in reflecting momentous political incidents and the kaleidoscopic events of social life. Most of them voiced opposition to the foreign invasion and exposed the evil feudal system of the day.

The best-known poets of this period are Gong Zizhen（龚自珍，1792 A.D.—1840 A.D.）, Huang Zunxian（黄遵宪，1848 A.D.—1905 A.D.）and Liu Yazi（柳亚子，1887 A.D.—1958 A.D.）. Gong Zizhen was one of the founders of modern Chinese literature. He was a progressive as well as a creative romantic poet. He inherited and developed the tradition of romanticism. His poems are brilliant in style, bright in diction, and resonant with sound and emotions, bearing striking characteristics as different from his romantic predecessors. His works are collected into *The Complete Works of Gong Dingan*（《龚定庵全集》）, with *Poems 1839*（《己亥杂诗》）being the most famous. Huang Zunxian's poems vividly reflect the effects of modern capitalist materialism as well as spiritual advancements upon the social life and the people's thoughts and feelings. In his description of the outside world, the poet displays the fresh experience and reflection of China's first intellectuals going abroad. Liu Yazi was one of the founders of the Southern Society, China's first modern revolutionary literary society. His poems are passionate and imbued with patriotism. Other distinguished poets include Wei Yuan（魏源，1794 A.D.—1857 A.D.）, Lin Zexu（林则徐，1785 A.D.—1850 A.D.）, Kang Youwei（康有为，1858 A.D.—1927 A.D.）, Tan Sitong（谭嗣同，1865 A.D.—1898 A.D.）and Qiu Jin（秋瑾，1875 A.D.—1907 A.D.）.

Novels were also flourishing during this period and over 1,000 appeared. Most renowned are:

Exposure of the Official World（《官场现形记》）

Written by Li Boyuan（李伯元，1867 A.D.—1906 A.D.）of the Qing Dynasty, *Exposure of the Official World*（also translated as *The True Colors of Officialism*）reveals and condemns the darkness of the Qing officialdom and aims to rescue the country. The book strips away the solemn and magnificent disguise of officialism and exposes its dirty and base original form. Like the slave society, the feudal society focused on officials（官本位）and was ruled by officials. The officialdom was the most dirty and evil place.

The Travel Records of Lao Can（《老残游记》）

Liu E's（刘鹗，1857 A.D.—1909 A.D.）*The Travel Records of Lao Can* was a renowned novel at the end of Qing Dynasty. The 20-chapter book features an old quack doctor and is based upon what he sees and hears during his travels, weaving startling stories of the tyranny and meanness of the Qing officialdom.

Flowers in a Mirror（《镜花缘》）

Flowers in a Mirror is a novel written by Li Ruzhen（李汝珍，1763 A.D.—1830 A.D.）in the Qing Dynasty. The 100-chapter novel tells of Tang Ao's（唐敖）travels in overseas regions and the stories of 100 talented female scholars. The author employs satirical caricature to ridicule the ugly social practice of his time. Between the lines, readers can envision the dog heads of the people in the Dog Nation and other images, which are full of irony against a real backdrop. From time to time, the author develops an artistic style by harmonizing irony and humor.

Chinese bourgeoisie felt the need to learn from the West as contacts with foreign countries increased daily. Over 1,000 western novels were translated during this period, playing a part in promoting Chinese fiction-writing of the time and subsequent years. The leading translators were Yan Fu（严复，1853 A.D.—1921 A.D.）and Lin Shu（林纾，1852 A.D.—1924 A.D.）.

The Rise and Development of Revolutionary Literature

On May 4th, 1919 an anti-imperialist, anti-feudal revolutionary movement broke out, marking the beginning of a revolutionary literature. The aims of the May 4th Movement were to promote science, democracy and writing in the vernacular（白话文），and this directly helped the development of the new literary movement.

Lu Xun（鲁迅，1881 A.D.—1936 A.D.），the chief figure of this cultural revolution, laid down the cornerstone for this movement. With incisive realism, his collections of essays such as *Call to Arms*（《投枪集》）and *Wandering*（《彷徨》）lash out against the iniquities of the time. His short story *The True Story of Ah Q*（《阿Q正传》）is internationally acknowledged as an immortal work in the history of modern Chinese literature. *The Goddesses*（《女神》）by Guo Moruo（郭沫若，1892 A.D.—1978 A.D.）is an outstanding example of modern Chinese poetry. With the founding of the Chinese Communist Party in 1921, the proletariat came forward in the new literary movement. In order to unite progressive writers and oppose the Kuomintang's "encirclement and suppression" policies, the China League of Left-wing Writers（左翼作家联盟）led by the Communist Party was established in March, 1930, and the magazine *The Dipper*（《拓荒者》）and *Literature Monthly*（《革命月刊》）were inaugurated. It was during this period that Lu Xun, influenced by Marxism, fought against the reactionaries with his trenchant polemic essays, becoming a giant in China's cultural revolution. Jiang Guangchi's（蒋光赤，1901 A.D.—1931 A.D.）poems and his novel *Wind That Blows Across the Fields*（《田野的风》）, Yin Fu's（殷夫，1909 A.D.—1931 A.D.） poems and Hu Yeping's（胡也平，1905 A.D.—1931 A.D.）novel *Light Is Before Us*（《光明在前》）, all describe the popular struggle led by the Party against imperialism and feudalism, clearly indicating the growth of proletarian literature. Other important works of this period are Mao Dun's（茅盾，1896 A.D.—1981 A.D.）novel *Midnight*（《子夜》）, Lao She's（老舍，1899 A.D.—1966 A.D.）novel *Camel Xiangzi*（《骆驼祥子》）, Ba Jin's（巴金，1904 A.D.—2005 A.D.） *Trilogy of the Turbulent Currents*（《激流三部曲》） embracing three full-length novels — *The Family*（《家》）, *Spring*（《春》） and *Autumn*（《秋》）and Cao Yu's（曹禺，1910 A.D.—1996 A.D.） play *Thunderstorm*（《雷雨》）.

In May 1942, during the anti-Japanese War, Chairman Mao Zedong made *A Speech at Yan'an Forum on Literature and Art*（《在延安文艺座谈会上的讲话》）, which became a torch guiding the writers and artists to go among the masses to familiarize themselves with their lives and struggles. As a result, a great number of fine works were produced, such as Zhao Shuli's（赵树理，1906 A.D.—1970 A.D.）novel *The Marriage of Young Black*（《小二黑结婚》） and *Rhymes of Li Youcai*（《李有才板话》）, Li Ji's（李季，1922 A.D.—1980 A.D.）long poem *Wang Gui and Li Xiangxiang*（《王贵与李香香》）and the opera *The White-haired Girl*（《白毛女》） by He Jingzhi（贺敬之，1924 A.D.— ） and Ding Yi（丁毅，1920 A.D.—1998 A.D.）. *The Hurricane*（《暴风骤雨》）, a novel by Zhou Libo（周立波，1908 A.D.—1979 A.D.）, was famous during the War of Liberation, which truthfully portrays the Chinese peasants' struggle for overthrowing the feudal rule and abolishing the system of exploitation.

Contemporary Literature（当代文学，1919 A.D.— ）

In my opinion, the Chinese contemporary literature can be divided into the following periods:

The first period is from the May 4th Movement in 1919 to the founding of the People's Republic of China in 1949. In the eventful 30 years there appeared many great writers and important works. The contingent of writers in this period consists of two groups: those of the older generation who made great contribution to the development of new Chinese literature during the May 4th Movement in 1919 and the activities of the League of Left-wing Writers in 1930s, such as Lu Xun, Guo Moruo, Mao Dun, Ba Jin, Lao She, Tian Han and others; those who distinguished themselves not long after the Yan'an forum on literature and art, such as Zhao Shuli, Zhou Libo, Liu Qing（柳青，1916 A.D.—1978 A.D.）, Ai Qing（艾青，1910 A.D.—1996 A.D.）, Ding Ling（丁玲，1907 A.D.—1986 A.D.），

He Jingzhi, Li Ji and others.

The second period is from the founding of the People's Republic of China in 1949 to the beginning of the cultural revolution in 1966. In this period of 17 years, there appeared a multitude of writers and works under the impetus of the founding of the new republic and the beginning of a new life, such as Wei Wei(魏巍, 1920 A.D.—2008 A.D.), Du Pengcheng(杜鹏程, 1921 A.D.—1991 A.D.), Guo Xiaochuan(郭小川, 1919 A.D.—1976 A.D.), Liang Bin(梁斌, 1914 A.D.—1996 A.D.), Qu Bo(曲波, 1923 A.D.—2002 A.D.). Yang Mo(杨沫, 1914 A.D.—1995 A.D.), Li Zhun(李准, 1928 A.D.—2000 A.D.) and others.

Most of their works depict the nation's socialist transformation and construction. Examples of these are Liang Bin's *Builders*(《创业史》), Zhou Libo's *Great Changes in a Mountain Village*(《山乡巨变》), Zhao Shuli's *Sanliwan Village*(《山里湾》) and Du Pengcheng's *Steeled and Tempered*(《百炼成钢》). Many works take their themes from China's revolutionary history and struggles, such as Qu Bo's *Tracks in the Snowy Forest*(《林海雪原》), Yang Mo's *The Song of Youth*(《青春之歌》), Luo Guangbin(罗广斌, 1924 A.D.—1967 A.D.) and Yang Yiyan's(杨益言, 1925 A.D.—2017 A.D.) *Red Crag*(《红岩》).

In addition, a number of writers of minority nationalities have come to the fore—Malaqinhu(玛拉沁夫, Mongolian, 1930 A.D.—), author of the novel *On the Boundless Grassland*(《茫茫的大草原》); Li Qiao(李乔, Yi, 1909 A.D.—2002 A.D.), author of the novel *The Joyful Golden Sand River*(《欢笑的金沙江》)and Wei Qilin(韦其麟, Zhuang, 1935 A.D.—), author of the long poem *Hundred-Bird Dress*(《百鸟衣》).

In the field of traditional operas, the scripts of *Fifteen Strings of Cash*(《十五贯》) and *The Monkey King Subdues the Demon*(《孙悟空三打白骨精》) have been re-edited and improved before being put into book form. Many narrative poems and legends of minority nationalities like *Ashma*(《阿诗玛》) and *Third Sister Liu*(《刘三姐》) have been adapted into operas or films and are widely acclaimed.

The third period is the so-called the "Great Cultural Revolution" from 1966 to 1976, which is a period of cultural desert. Chinese people at that time had nothing to read but could only see the "eight model revolutionary operas."

The fourth period begins with the downfall of the "Gang of Four" (四人帮) in 1976 and the carrying out of the policy "Reform and Opening to the Outside" in 1979. It is a period of great significance in Chinese history. Great changes have taken place in the political circle and the economic structure. China is experiencing the transition from a planned economy to a market economy, with a rapid development in economy, culture and science. People's concept of value, and their attitude towards life have taken dramatic turns. So many significant works appeared in this period, which, however, are beyond my power to make estimation and give comments. So I'll leave them to those talented critics.

· *Presentation* ·

Give a presentation on one of the periods of Chinese Literature or on one of the great writers and his / her masterpiece.

Ⅲ

Six Arts and Four Treasures of the Studio in Ancient China

Six Arts

From the Western Zhou to the mid Spring and Autumn Period, scholars were primary teachers in the "government schools"（官学）, offering instruction to the children of the nobles on "Six Arts", namely *Li*（礼） Meaning rites and manners; *Yue*（乐）, music and dance; *She*（射）, archery; *Yu*（御）, wagon-driving; *Shu*（书）, character recognition and writing; and *Shu*（数）, arithmetic. These were jointly called "Small Arts"（小艺）for the beginners.

There were also senior instructors in the schools who were called *Shi*（师） meaning teachers, who taught youngsters what we call "Grand Arts"（大艺）: *Book of Odes*（《诗经》）, *Book of History*（《尚书》）, *Book of Changes*（《周易》）, *Spring and Autumn Annals*（《春秋》）, *Book of Rites*（《礼记》） and *Book of Music*（《乐》）, jointly known as the Six Classics（六经）. The teachers were respected for their expertise, and for this reason, other learned men also assumed the title of "scholars"（儒）.

From the "Small Arts," we know the reasonable framework of ancient education, which did not only lay emphasis on learning, i.e. to recognize words and to learn to write, but also on paying attention to practical skills as well as physical training. *Li*（礼）is learned for future social dealings. *Yue*（乐）is to cultivate the children's personality. *She*（射） and *Yu*（御）are practical skills which can also be regarded as kinds of physical training.

Four Treasures of the Studio

Today, pen, ink and paper are stationery in the studio. But in ancient China, we had brushes and inksticks instead of pen and ink. *Hu* brushes（湖笔）, *Hui* inksticks（徽墨）, *Xuan* paper（宣纸） and *Duan* inkstones（端砚） were popularly known as "the Four Treasures of the Studio,"（文房四宝） for they were of high quality and essential for calligraphy and painting.

Hu brushes were made as early as the 3rd century B.C.E. in Hu Preferture（湖州）, of Zhejiang Province, hence the name. The Hu brush, made from the hair of Hu goat, featured itself for its roundness（园）, neatness（齐）, strongness（健）and pointedness（尖）. People called it Hu Yin（湖颖）. With a long history, it was very well-known both at home and abroad.

Hui inksticks were produced in Hui Prefecture（徽州, nowadays Huangshan City, Anhui Province）. It was said the ink "took to paper like paint and lasted one thousand years."（落纸如漆，万载存真。）The Anhui's inksticks were made of the ashes of burnt green pine from the Huangshan Mountain, mixed with a kind of glue. Then they were put in *Nanmu*（楠木）wood moulds and carved with scenes of pavilions, pagodas, hills, brooks, plants, birds and beasts.

Xuan paper was first produced in Jingxian County（泾县）of today's Anhui Province. The county belonged to *Xuan* Prefecture（宣州）in the Tang Dynasty, hence its name *xuanzhi*（宣纸）. In ancient China, people used bamboo strips and silk for writing, one heavy and the other expensive. The production of *Xuan* paper was especially precious for calligraphy and painting. Made in an 18-step process from the bark of wingceltis and rice straw, the paper was white and soft, durable and absorbent, which made it "lasting a thousand years"（纸寿千年）.

Duan inkstones, first produced in Duanzhou（端州）, Guangdong Province, were made from the stones found at the bottom of a mountain stream called "Duan Xi"（端溪）. They had a fine, solid texture and glossy sheen, and ink prepared in them did not dry quickly. Carved into various shapes and designs, the inkstone served as a fine desk ornament besides its function as a tool for writing and painting.

· *Seminar* ·

1. Comment on the Six Arts and Six Classics.
2. Make an advertisement on one of the Four Treasures of the Studio.

IV
Calligraphy and Painting

Calligraphy and painting are regarded as two treasured arts in China. Together with *qin*（琴, the ancient *Zheng* 古筝）and *qi*（棋, chess）, they formed the four skills for a learned scholar to pursue in ancient China. They were also held as a good exercise to temper one's character and cultivate one's personality.

Calligraphy

Calligraphy has been regarded as a form of visual art through the ages in China. A fine piece of calligraphy, known as *Mobao*(墨宝—a treasure in ink), is often more treasured by a collector of art than a good painting. It sells well on the market. For thousands of years, children began learning calligraphy as soon as they entered school at an early age.

It is deep-rooted in the Chinese mind that a person's personality manifested itself through his/her handwriting.

The art of Chinese calligraphy arose mainly from the shape and structure of the Chinese characters and the use of Chinese blush which is also good for painting. The earliest Chinese characters are called *Jiaguwen*(甲骨文), i.e. inscriptions on tortoise shells and animal bones of the Shang Dynasty. They are pictographs(象形文字). Though varied in size, shape and structure, each of the characters has a balanced and symmetrical pattern. These early characters, graceful in themselves, laid down the foundation for the art of Chinese calligraphy.

In the Qin Dynasty, Qin Shihuang standardized the Chinese characters—the whole empire used only one script called *Xiaozhuan*(小篆), a style often used in seals, which is beautiful in shape and structure.

In the Han Dynasty since this seal style of writing was not convenient, a new style of writing called *Lishu*(隶书)was invented on the basis of the preceding one, which used construction of dashes(撇)and dots(点), and horizontal(横)and vertical(竖)strokes, adding charm to the handwriting. This style of writing soon became the official script in the Han Dynasty.

By the end of the Eastern Han a new style was invented, called *Caoshu*(草书) with strokes flowing and characters linking together. This style of calligraphy looked more smooth and lively. Also in this period, another calligraphy called *Xingshu*(行书 running hand) was used, which wrote in a simpler and faster way.

During the period from the Three Kingdoms through the Western and Eastern Jin Dynasties to the Southern and Northern Dynasties, Chinese calligraphy made further advance. On the basis of *Lishu*, a new style called *Kaishu*(楷书, regular script) was invented. With its strokes looking both vigorous and soft, *Kaishu* had many good characteristics and was generally liked by the intelligentsia and the masses as well, laying the foundation for the written form of the modern Chinese language.

In the Eastern Jin Dynasty, there appeared one of the greatest Chinese calligraphers, Wang Xizhi(王羲之 , 321 A.D.—379 A.D.), who, by absorbing the essence of the art of Chinese calligraphy since the Han Dynasty, developed a new style of his own and reached a very high level of artistic achievement in the running hand and cursive hand. He was respected as the "master of calligraphy," and his hand-writing influenced many later calligraphers.

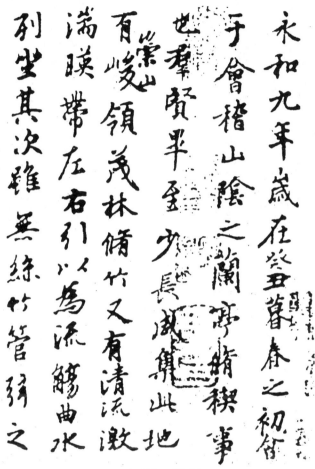

by Wang Xizhi

Calligraphy flourished during the Sui and Tang Dynasties. Great calligraphers appeared one after another, among them Zhang Xu（张旭, 675 A.D.—750 A.D.）, Yan Zhenqing（颜真卿, 709 A.D.—785 A.D.）, Liu Gongquan（柳公权, 778 A.D.—865 A.D.）, and the monk Huai Su（怀素, 725 A.D.—785 A.D.）were unique and influential. Zhang Xu was best known for his cursive handwriting, gaining the title of "master of the cursive hand." Yan Zhenqing invented the stately and imposing "Yan Style"（颜体）. Liu Gongquan at first learned from Yan, but later dropped Yan's characteristics of "bold and fat" strokes and developed a style with "thin and hard" strokes and the two men's styles were vividly described by later generations as the "Yan muscles and Liu bones." The monk Huai Su was good at cursive hand, but his calligraphy was wilder than Zhang Xu's and was therefore termed "wild cursive hand"（狂草）.

by Yan Zhengqing

by Zhang Xu

Calligraphy in the Song and Yuan Dynasties paled beside that of the Tang, but still we had some noted calligraphers like Su Shi（苏轼，1037 A.D.—1101 A.D.），Huang Tingjian（黄庭坚，1045 A.D.—1105 A.D.）and others. During the Ming and the Qing Dynasties, calligraphy in China made great progress again. This is because the art of painting flourished in the Ming Dynasty and gave impetus to the development of calligraphy since these two art forms are closely associated.

In modern times, because of the invention of other writing instruments, such as pen, pencil and ball-pen, which are convenient and soon gained popularity, Chinese calligraphy lost, to a great extent, its value of practical use and gradually became a pure artistic form. But there are still quite a lot of people among the population, especially the older generation, who love this art and keep practising it all their lives. All over China, decorative calligraphy can be found everywhere, especially in temples and pagodas, on the walls of caves, and the sides of mountains and monuments.

By using simple lines to convey a complex artistic conception or temperament, this special art of China has aroused the interest of more and more artists home and abroad.

Painting

Traditional Chinese painting is highly regarded the world over for its original style and distinctive national features. Over the centuries, the practice of countless artists has made this traditional Chinese painting what it is now—an art subdivided into a multitude of schools all with some traits in common.

In terms of mode of expression, traditional Chinese painting falls into two categories:

The *Xieyi*（写意, literally "painting the feeling"）school, marked by exaggeration of form and liberal use of ink; and the *Gongbi*（工笔, or "meticulous brushwork"）school, characterized by strict and detailed representation of the subject.

Xieyi is a fundamental approach to the Chinese pictorial art. It consists of an aesthetic system entirely different from that of the West. "Depicting the sentiments" is a concept directly opposite to that of "depicting reality." Chinese painting has passed through a long process of evolution since it originated as the depiction of reality. For more than a thousand years, Chinese painters have not been content to limit their works to the bounds set by reality. Gu Kaizhi（顾恺之, 345 A.D.—406 A.D.）was the first to express this as a theory, known as "using the form to express the spirit"（以形传神）. He maintained that a picture should serve as a means to show not only the appearance of a thing, but the artist's viewpoint on it as well. This can be said to be a statement of the dialectical relationship between form and spirit in Chinese painting.

The experience of the painter is enshrined in the phrase "*Qiyun*"（气韵）. "*Qi*" is cosmic spirit, literally Meaning "breath" or "vapour" that vitalizes all things and gives life and growth to them. It is the task of the artist to attune himself to this cosmic spirit and let it infuse him with energy so that in a moment of inspiration, he may become the vehicle for its expression. Later there appeared such theories as "likeness in spirit resides in unlikeness." This viewpoint, particular to traditional Chinese painting, differs considerably from the convention frequently associated in China with Western painting which places resemblance of form above all else. Hence Chinese painting is less subjected to the limitation of proportion, anatomy, perspective and light. The pictures created by the brush of a skilled artist are not the specific images of the object in nature, but rather their essence grasped and transformed by means of a masterly technique based on a profound recognition and understanding of the subject. To the artist, images are more important than reality, and moving objects than static ones.

"Taking nature as one's teacher, and the heart as a source of inspiration" and "go to the imagination to depict the marvelous" — these are other important theories in Chinese pictorial creation. Here, beyond the representation of the subject and its spirit, one perceives an emphasis on expressing the painter's self and his thinking. He paints not only what he sees and feels but what he imagines. In this sense, the high degree of abstraction and stylization in Chinese painting is the result of profound observation of nature and, after discarding everything redundant, the expression of its essence in an exaggerated manner.

In subject matter, the most popular ones have been landscapes, human figures, animals, fishes, birds and flowers—the last two being frequently combined as "flower and bird painting" (花鸟画). Figure painting, which reached maturity during the Warring States Period, flourished against a Confucian background, illustrating moralistic themes. From the Han Dynasty to the end of the Tang Dynasty, the human figure occupied the dominant position in Chinese painting, as it did in pre-modern European art.

flower and bird painting   landscape painting

Landscape painting is called *shanshui hua* (山水画) in Chinese. *Shanshui* Means mountains and rivers, which stand for nature. Landscape painting is thus called because mountain and water occupy the most important place in a piece of landscape painting, while non-essential elements of landscape and people are either omitted or painted as embellishment. Nature is predominant, and human beings are only part of it. This concept of man's relationship with nature was especially executed in the paintings of the Song Dynasty, which greatly influenced later landscape painters up to the present.

The symbolism used in Chinese landscape painting often puzzles the Western eye. Mountains, rivers, plants, animals, birds, flowers, etc., can all be chosen for their traditional association as much as for their inherent beauty. The pine, for example, represents uprightness and immortality. It is one of the trio of plants which are generally called the "three friends of winter" (岁寒三友), the other two being bamboo and prunes. The orchid, a modest flower, is often identified with the high principles of the unassertive scholar or artist. Another much depicted group of flowers are the "flowers of the four seasons." They are the peony, standing for riches and honors; the lotus, coming out of the mire without being smeared, for purity; the chrysanthemum, for elegance, righteousness and longevity; and the prunes, for bravery, besides, it is also regarded as the messenger of spring. The bird crane is believed to live a long life. The fish, pronounced *Yu* in Chinese, stands for plenty.

Chinese painting is one of the treasures in oriental art. With a typical national character and a splendid tradition, Chinese painting occupies a unique place in the history of world art.

1. How did the Chinese calligraphy come into being?

2. What is the theory of *Xieyi*（写意）in traditional Chinese painting?

V

Acrobatic Art, Martial Arts, Taiji Quan and Qigong

Acrobatic Art（杂技）

performance by a Wuqiao acrobatic troupe

As one of the art forms, acrobatics has long been popular among the Chinese people for more than two thousand years. As early as the Warring States Period, there appeared rudiments of acrobatics. By the time of the Han Dynasty, the acrobatic art further developed both in content and form and there appeared superb performances with music accompaniment on the stage, such as "Pole climbing," "Rope-walking," "Fish turned into Dragon" (the present day "Conjuring"), "Five tables" (like today's balance on chairs), etc. In the Tang Dynasty, the most thriving period in ancient China, the number of acrobats greatly increased and their performing skills much improved. In the Dunhuang mural paintings（敦煌壁画）, there are images of acrobatic and circus performers.

In the long course of development, the Chinese acrobatic art has formed its own style. The ancient acrobatics stemmed from people's life and labor. Tools of labor like tridents, wicker rings and articles of daily life such as tables, chairs, jars, plates and bowls were used in their performances. At festivals, people often performed "Flying trident," "Balance on chair," "Jar Tricks," "Hoop diving," "Lion dance" at the market places or in the streets of the town.

After 1949, the acrobatic art has not only made great improvement in its contents and skill but has also set up a designing and directing system, aiming at creating graceful stage images, harmonious musical accompaniment, and good supporting effects of costumes, props and lighting. The present Chinese acrobatics is full of optimism and well reflects the industry, resourcefulness, courage and undauntedness of the Chinese people. In the past fifty years, many Chinese acrobatic troupes have toured more than one hundred countries and regions around the world and won dozens of gold or silver medals in the international acrobatic festivals and championships.

Wuqiao（吴桥）, a county on the bank of the Grand Canal in Hebei Province is renowned as the homeland of acrobatics in China. It is said that all the people in Wuqiao, from toddlers learning to walk to centenarians, can perform some kind of acrobatic art. Young people especially practise the art during their breaks from labor in the fields. Many families have their unique skills passed down through generations. In Wuqiao, one might find a farmer in the threshing area balancing a handcart on his chin; a child walking along the road balancing an inverted bottle filled with oil or vinegar on his little finger; or a pupil on the way to school on a rainy day balancing an umbrella on his head. There are many acrobats from Wuqiao throughout China and the world. There is an old saying in the Chinese acrobatic circle: "If you don't have an acrobat from Wuqiao, you can't have an acrobatic troupe."

Martial Arts

martial arts

Martial arts, also called *Wushu*（武术）or *Gongfu*（功夫）in Chinese, are popular sports in China. It is loved and practised by people of all ages. It needs practically no equipment— just an opening of a few square metres. It has been used for treating illness and strengthening the physique as well as for self-defense through generations.

Martial arts originated from the human activities of production and pursuit for survival in primeval times. Menaced by wild animals in hunting, the primitive people developed some armed and unarmed grappling techniques（擒拿术）, using simple weapons and devices, such as hitting, dodging, jumping, chopping and stabbing, to capture the game as well as for self-defence. In slave and feudal societies, martial arts were also used for military purposes, forming complete systems for offense and defence. Martial arts reached a height during the Tang and Song Dynasties. The rulers of the Tang Dynasty implemented the system of selecting military commanders through imperial military competitions and encouraged martial art practice by conferring prizes and titles to the winners. The Song Dynasty widely promoted martial arts and set up military schools, training warriors with the combat techniques. Many military generals were great martial art masters. In the time of peace, they taught martial arts to their soldiers so as to increase their combat effectiveness. It is also in the Song Dynasty that many martial art societies were set up and every martial art routine was perfected with a beginning and a closing form.

There are various martial art schools in China, such as boxing including *Taiji Quan*, *Shaolin Quan*, *Nan Quan*, *Xiangxing Quan* (which imitates the movements of animals), *Drunken Quan*, etc., and *Qigong* (breathing exercises), including *Yinggong* (硬功) through which people will be able to withstand or exert an enormous force.

Since martial arts are combative and attack-oriented and the slight negligence could lead to bloodshed and death, the Chinese martial arts lay special emphasis on martial ethics, setting up a complete set of moral codes. "Strive for morality rather than strength," "One must refine one's morals before practising martial arts" are the mottoes among the martial art circles. Almost all martial art schools throughout history have considered morality their top priority, enforcing strict moral standards. For example, Shaolin Temple, one of the most famous martial art bases, stipulates that disciples should be carefully selected, and the skills can be taught only to upright and moral people. The Wudang School stipulates that people who are involved in adultery, robbery, vice, prostitution or gambling violate the school's code of conduct.

The following are the essential points of Chinese martial art ethics: pursuing truth and goodness; displaying brotherhood, righteousness, honesty and fairness; emphasizing moral conduct and good manners; respecting the teacher and loyal to his school; stressing modesty, magnanimity and freedom from personal grudges; and emphasizing persistence and perseverance in learning the arts.

Taiji Quan

Today, if you take an early morning walk in the cities or towns of China, you will see people practising *Taiji Quan* in parks, on the sidewalks and opening areas. Why is *Taiji Quan* so deeply loved and widely practised by the Chinese people? Let's have a study of its theory and principles.

Taiji (the great ultimate), one of the essential concepts of the ancient Chinese philosophy on the world system, first appeared in the *Book of Changes*. "Where there is *Taiji*, there is peace and harmony between the positive and the negative." *Taiji* theory holds that everything in the world is composed of two opposing but complementary aspects, *Yin* (阴) and *Yang* (阳). The *Yang* is described as masculine in character—active, warm,

dry, bright, procreative and positive. It is seen in the sun, the fire, in anything with heat in it, representing the male property of all kinds. The *Yin* is an energy mode in a lower and slower key, which is the female or negative principle in nature, fertile, breeding, dark, cold, wet, secret, and mysterious. It is seen in shadows, in quiescent things. A single object may at one moment show *Yin* characteristics and at another become a *Yang* object aflame with energy. For instance, a dried-out log is to all appearance *Yin* in character, but if put in a fire, it will prove to have *Yang* qualities in abundance.

This theory has been demonstrated in the famous *Taiji* Chart which, known as "the illustration of the motion of the world," shows symbolically the balance and coexistence of these two energies, *Yin* and *Yang*.

The black in the chart stands for *Yin* and the white for *Yang*. The *Yin* fish and the *Yang* fish revolve around, chasing each other, a representation of the principle of unceasing motion and change. The coexistence of the two fish in the same circle indicates that the *Yin* and *Yang* forces are present in everything. A black spot in the white fish and a white one in the black fish stand for the embrace of *Yin* and *Yang* within each other.

Originating from the roots of classical Chinese culture, *Taiji Quan* absorbed a variety of sources—the *Book of Changes*, Taoism and Buddhism in its development and gradually formed a complete set of graceful and stylized movements. To a Westerner seeing *Taiji Quan* for the first time, it looks like a ballet in slow motion. It consists of a sequence of forms involving every part of the body and executed in a highly stylized yet natural manner. You stand straight but not stiff. Your body is supple but not limp. Your movements are slow but steady, poised and powerful. After a period of exercising, you can train yourself to be physically as soft as an infant, as resilient as a twig in the wind, sensitive to the slightest pressure on any part of your body, and mentally alert.

First of all, *Taiji Quan* lays emphasis on the concentration of the mind. It is believed that mental concentration can mobilize an internal energy current which in turn guides the physical movements. In other words, the movements are no longer the results of conscious physical effort but the effect of mental concentration. The performer possesses a unity of tranquillity and motion. It is both mental and physical exercises. That's why *Taiji Quan* can benefit the function of the central nerous system and cure neurasthenia.

A second basic principle is synchronization of the movement. Physically all movements involve every part of the body, though each emphasizes some specific part. The whole *Taiji Quan* sequence unfolds itself in an uninterrupted continuity. The body is naturally extended and relaxed with the hands, eyes, limbs performing with the body as a whole. The performers should not concentrate his or her attention on one part of the body and neglect the other.

While *Taiji Quan* is basically an exercise for health, its various forms are designed for self-defence. The foremost principle is never to attack first and when being attacked, never to counter force with force but instead to make use of the attacking force to defeat the attacker. Suppose a man throws a punch at you, instead of countering it, you dodge and grab his fist and throw him in the direction of his motion. That is what some practitioners called "subduing the vigorous by the soft" and "overcoming a weight of one thousand *jin*（斤）by four *liang*（两）".

Because it requires natural and deep breathing, and smooth, rhythmic and balanced movements, *Taiji Quan* exercises can also increase the elasticity of the lung tissues and strengthen the bones, muscles and joints. These characteristics are important factors contributing to the prevention and curing of many diseases such as high blood pressure, neurasthenia and tuberculosis.

Taiji Quan, both as an exercise and as an art of self-defence, reflects a way of life, a philosophy. The standing posture and the movements symbolize a personality of straightforwardness and integrity, serenity and dignity. They indicate a man of mental balance and emotional stability as well as physical well-being. The emphasis on suppleness and resilience points to a friendly disposition and absence of aggressiveness. The coordination and synchronization of movements illustrate a basic attitude towards one's work and responsibility.

In summary, *Taiji Quan* aims at developing a wholesome man (within himself), a friendly man (towards others), a conscientious man (about his work and his responsibility), a man at peace with himself and with the world.

Qigong

Mysterious and wondrous, *Qigong* is an outstanding legacy of Chinese culture as well as an important part of traditional Chinese medicine. As a form of traditional breathing exercise, *Qigong* has been used by the Chinese people for thousands of years to prevent and cure diseases, strengthen the constitution, avoid premature aging and prolong life.

Literally *Qi*（气）Means "air" or "breath," in fact, it refers to the body's physiological functions. *Qigong* experts call it internal *Qi* or *dantian*（丹田）*Qi*(mainly from the visceral organs) which generate life. In ancient Chinese cosmology, *Qi* is closely tied in with "spirit" as distinguished from "physical substance." The Taoist philosophy regards man's *Qi* as part of the universal *Qi* or man's life-force. *Gong* refers to *Gongfu*（功夫, practising skills）. Therefore, *Qigong* is a kind of self-training method by which the practitioner uses the initiative to train the body and mind, providing a holistic training for self-reliance, self-adjustment, body building, prophylaxis, curing diseases and strengthening the constitution, resisting premature aging and prolonging life.

In prophylaxis and treating diseases, *Qigong* exerts effects on the body through its required movements, postures, regulation of respiration and control of thought, building up constitution and strengthening bodily resistence. It has been proved to be effective in treating some chronic diseases, especially hypertension, coronary heart disease, ulcers, neurasthenia and bronchitis. *Qigong* can reduce severity of disease and promote earlier recovery without any special equipment. So it is highly desirable to employ *Qigong* clinically.

Qigong is also effective for body building. People who keep practising *Qigong* usually enjoy the benefits of improved digestion and respiration, cardiovascular and nervous systems. It improves sleep quality, relieves fatigue, strengthens physical and mental conditions, enhances stamina and thus improves working efficiency.

Frolics of Five Animals

Qigong also brings anti-aging and life-prolonging effects. In ancient times, people believed that *Qigong* was a method for curing diseases and prolonging life. Some even regarded it as the key to immortality. According to historical records, Hua Tuo（华佗）, a famous doctor of the Three Kingdoms Period, invented the Frolics of Five Animals（五禽戏） exercises. He persisted in practising it. As a result, he looked young at the age of one hundred. This youth-preserving effects are verified by the aged who have practised long-term *Qigong* exercise. Most people who persist in *Qigong* exercise are spirited with normal blood pressure, have good vision and hearing, have ringing voices, and sound teeth, and can sleep well, walk with firm strides, withstand the heat or cold, and seldom suffer from diseases; they differ greatly from those taking little exercise. So *Qigong* contributes greatly to geriatrics.

There are numerous kinds of *Qigong* exercises, each with its own features and effects, differing according to posture, method, form, style and purpose. At present, there are nearly four hundred kinds of *Qigong* exercises in China. Roughly, *Qigong* can be divided into two main forms: "hard *Qigong*," also called martial art or *Gongfu*, and "soft *Qigong*" which includes health-building and therapeutic *Qigong*. *Qigong* can also be classified into quiescent *Qigong*（静功）, dynamic *Qigong*（动功） and emitting *Qigong*（发功）.

Generally, there are four main postures in *Qigong* exercises, namely, lying, sitting, standing and walking. Although there are various ways to practise *Qigong*, the following three are essential, i.e., "regulating the mind," "regulating the body" and "regulating the breath."

Regulating the mind into a state of tranquillity, or "calming the mind," is the most fundamental skill in *Qigong* practice. This method was also called "heart-regulation" in ancient China. Calm the mind and avoid worrying about worldly cares, and then *Zhen Qi* (Essential Qi) will be able to travel smoothly along the channels and the body will not be invaded by diseases. In modern medical terms, this method can induce the activity of the cerebral cortex which controls the brain and the rest of the body and relieve the cerebral cortex of pathological tension or excitation caused by certain illness, thus helping it to regain its power to regulate the function of the body.

Regulation of the body is also an important technique in *Qigong* practice. According to scientific experiments, the oxygen consumption and metabolic rate during *Qigong* practice are even lower than during a sound sleep, which is beneficial for reducing consumption of vital energy, allowing it to reaccumulate. In this way, *Qigong* exercise helps cure some chronic disease and strengthen health.

Regulating the breath, with the help of slow and smooth movements of the body, promotes circulation in the portal veins as well as in the systemic and pulmonary circulatory systems. The net result of this exercise is an increase in the vital capacity of the lung, improved functioning of the heart and stimulation of metabolism, thus creating favorable conditions for recovery of health.

It is generally believed that through "regulating the body," "regulating the mind," "regulating the breath," *Qigong* can increase vitality and promote longevity.

▼ Essentials of *Qigong* Exercises ◢

Even though there is such a variety of *Qigong* exercises, each with its own features and requirements, the general principles for them are the same: combination of relaxation, inward peace, natural movements, flow of *Qi*, integration of movements, quiescence, flexibility in the upper body and stability in the lower body, a moderate amount of exercise, and exercising in an orderly way.

Qigong relaxation entails the extremities and the whole body as well as a relaxed mental state. But it does not entail listlessness, slackness and rigidity. The quiescent state achieved by reflex conditioning is relative inward peace. While conscious, the brain continues working without stop. To relieve fatigue and restore energy, the brain needs to be in a quiescent state. However, this quiescence differs from the state of sleep or other kinds of rest because it requires a clear, focused mind. The quiescent state of *Qigong* does not mean complete stoppage of mental activities, but a state of relative quiet, or to say, a special state of inward quietude. Some people think that, after entering quiescence, nothing can be felt, and one even forgets one's existence. This is impossible. Entering quiescence during *Qigong* exercise is a directional exercise of mental activity during the awake state, In this state, the brain is aware of changes in physiological functions inside the body and maximally eliminates interference from both inside and outside the body. Some people feel like a frozen river melting during spring time after entering quiescence in which the whole body is completely relaxed and comfortable.

And then, how to enter quiescence? This is a common problem for beginners. It needs long-term practice. There are many methods for achieving quiescence. Those commonly used are focusing the mind on *dantian* (意守丹田), focusing the mind on the surrounding objects, counting the respiration, listening to respiration, reciting silently the words of catch sentences or verses, thinking about the Meanings of a word, and listening to light music or simple, pleasing sounds. Rid oneself of worries and concentrate on something to relax the mind. Achieving quiescence is actually mental training activity. The beginner may select a personally suitable method and repeat it to consolidate it into a conditioned reflex. Once the conditioned reflex is established, entering quiescence is easy. Do not set too strict a criterion for yourself, because it may lead to nervousness, in which it is impossible to enter quiescence. One must be relaxed physically and mentally to enter quiescence and keep the method simple. If it is too complicated, it will interfere with the process. So, for beginners, two points are necessary: the posture should be comfortable and only one method should be used to induce quiescence. Listening to the respiration or focusing the mind on *dantian* is good. If you feel uncomfortable due to your posture, adjust it slightly. Yet, the sound of respiration should be avoided during *Qigong* exercise. One should use *dantian* (the umbilicus) to listen to the sound of respiration.

As a remarkable scientific and cultural legacy, *Qigong* has performed great miracles in curing chronic diseases and building health. Many *Qigong* feats are marvelous and amazing, such as "splitting a stone with the head," "breaking a stone on the body that lies on daggers," "turning the body on a fork," etc. Some of the reasons for these *Qigong* feats can not be explained clearly yet, but from the perspective of modern physiology, the heart, muscles and brain all can produce a kind of bioelectricity. When the body is stimulated by a certain signal, bodily functions will be activated, as in an emergency, one may exert greater strength, run faster, or jump higher than normal. A *Qigong* master who has grasped the art of controling his *Qi* can coordinate his muscles, joints and visceral organs by a fleeting thought and concentrate all his *Qi* or vital energy on one point of the body so that it is usually dozens of times or even a hundred times more than an ordinary person can exert, thus able to render this area enormously strong and relatively insensitive to pain. Therefore, a *Qigong* master can split a stone with the head or hand by directing his *Qi* to those parts; when he directs his *Qi* to his throat, it can withstand a spear on the point; when he directs his *Qi* to his body, and it can support the weight of a car slowly running over without being injured.

The history of *Qigong* can be dated back to the Zhou Dynasty 3,000 years ago. *Qigong* exercises were already recorded in the *jinwen*（经文）texts, inscriptions on ancient bronze sacrificial objects. This kind of exercises was also described in the works of Lao Zi. The oldest book recording *Qigong* is Master Lu's *Spring and Autumn Annals* written in 230 B.C.E. In the *Yellow Emperor's Canon of Internal Medicine*（《黄帝内经》）, China's earliest medical works, written in the Warring States Period, the *Qigong* exercising method was also recorded. The Ming Dynasty medical expert Li Shizhen（李时珍,1518 A.D.—1593 A.D.）also mentioned *Qigong* in his works. Thus *Qigong* is an integral part of China's ancient cultural heritage which has contributed greatly and will continue to contribute to the health of the Chinese people as well as the people of the world.

· *Seminar* ·

1. What are the general principles of *Qigong*?
2. Try to enter quiescence in your spare time.

VI
Beijing Opera and Other Local Operas

Beijing Opera

Beijing Opera（formerly called Peking Opera）is regarded as the national opera in China and called "*Daxi*" （大戏, big drama）for it has a long history and a complete system of stage performance. Other local operas are called "*Xiaoxi*"（小戏, small drama）, usually developed from singing and story-telling mixed with folk songs and dances. By rough estimation, there are altogether about 360 types of traditional dramatic forms in China, Shaoxing Opera, Huangmei Opera, Ping Opera, Shanghai Opera, Guangdong Opera and Sichuan Opera being the most popular.

Beijing Opera was originally a local drama in Anhui Province. As the story goes, Emperor Qianlong of the Qing Dynasty fell interested in the local dramas during his inspection of the southern provinces in disguise. To celebrate his eightieth birthday in 1790, he summoned opera troupes from different localities to perform for him in Beijing. After the celebration, four famous troupes from Anhui Province were asked to remain. Audiences were particularly pleased with their beautiful melodies, colorful costumes and interesting facial patterns. Gradually it replaced *Kunqu*（昆曲） which had been popular in the palace and among the upper classes in Beijing. Later, some troupes from Hubei Province came to Beijing and often performed together with the Anhui troupes. The two types of singing blended on the same stage and gradually gave birth to a new genre which came to be known as Beijing Opera.

Beijing Opera absorbed the various elements of its forerunners—singing, dancing, mimicry and acrobatics, and adapted itself in language and style of singing to Beijing audiences. As time went by, its popularity spread all over the country, becoming the most popular and influential dramatic form on the Chinese stage.

The Roles of Beijing Opera

The characters of Beijing Opera are distinguished according to sex, age and disposition. They are customarily grouped into four types: *sheng*（生）, *dan*（旦）, *jing*（净） and *chou*（丑）.

Female roles are called *dan* which is further divided into *laodan*（老旦）— the elderly, dignified ladies, such as mothers and aunts; *qingyi*（青衣）—aristocratic ladies in elegant costumes; *huadan*（花旦）—ladies' maids, usually in colored costumes; *daoma dan*（刀马旦）, horsewomen and warriors; *choudan*（丑旦）, the wife of the *chou* role（丑角）, and sometimes shrewd and dangerous women. It is interesting that the *dan* role used to be performed by male actors. For instance, Mei Lanfang（梅兰芳）, one of the famous Beijing Opera actors was known for his performance of the *dan* role.

Male roles in Beijing Opera are either *sheng* or *chou*. The former are usually scholars, officials, etc., while the latter are clowns who can be easily recognized by their facial pattern—a patch of white around his eyes and nose, sometimes outlined in black. *Sheng* roles can be subdivided into *laosheng*（老生）and *xiaosheng*（小生）. The former being old men wearing long beards and the latter young men singing falsetto voice; as well as *wensheng*（文生）and *wusheng*（武生）, the former are scholars and officials and the latter are military officers in battle scenes and well trained in acrobatics. The *chou* or clowns, are usually foolish, awkward or stingy people.

The Facial Patterns and Costumes of Beijing Opera

The elaborate and gorgeous facial make-up and costumes are two distinguished characteristics of Beijing Opera. The audience knows from the colors and patterns what kind of character is being portrayed. For instance, red signifies honesty, probity, courage and bravery; purple does the same, but to a less degree; black indicates impartiality, fortitude, and sometimes coarseness and rudeness; blue stands for savageness and fierceness, yet sometimes arrogance; yellow symbolizes the same negative traits as blue, but milder; green is the color of unstable character. For example, the faces of devils are usually painted green; orange and gray are for old age; golden color is for gods, goddesses and emperors; good-natured people are usually painted with relatively simple colors while the make-up of hostile generals and doubtful characters, such as bandits, robbers, rebels and the like, bear complex marks.

The costuming of Beijing Opera is based mainly on the style of the Ming Dynasty court and civil costumes, with much use of deep red, deep green, yellow, white, black and blue. Strong contrasting colors are freely used, and embroidered in gold, silver and colored threads. The rules for costumes are strictly based on rank, occupation and life style; and there are special costumes with different colors and designs for each role.

The Music and Musical Instruments of Beijing Opera

The tunes of Beijing Opera are mainly composed of two styles: *erhuang*（二簧）and *xipi*（西皮）, the former originating in Hui tune（徽调）while the latter resulting from Han tune（汉调） in the Hubei Province. They are used according to the actions in different scenes. Generally speaking, the *xipi* tune is employed in lighter scenes while the *erhuang* for dramatic actions. Of course, some other tunes are also used for different purposes. The singing in Beijing Opera is highly stylized but its variations of rhythm and pitch enable the actors and actresses to express the thoughts and emotions of different characters in different situations. There are two forms of recitatives in dialogue and monologue: *yunbai*（韵白）—rhythmic vernacular and *jingbai*（京白）—capital vernacular, which are used to better characterize the personalities. Acting in Beijing Opera includes a set of movements, gestures and expressions. Every movement or pose, such as stroking a beard, setting a hat straight, swinging a sleeve or lifting a foot, has its own formula or pattern.

The most important of musical instruments used for the accompaniment to Beijing Opera is *jinghu*（京胡）, a kind of two-stringed fiddle followed by *erhu*（二胡）, also a two-stringed fiddle but in a soft tune. Other instruments include *yueqin*（月琴）, *pipa*（琵琶）and *suona*（唢呐）, etc. The percussion instruments are gongs and drums of different sizes, and castanets（响板）made of wood and bamboo. The castanets play an important role in making the temper. They are the "time-beater," and the whole orchestra is virtually directed by them. With the aid of gongs and drums, they beat the time for the actor, regulate his motions, give him his cue, etc.

The art of illusion is one of Beijing Opera's most important characteristics, expressed through techniques of exaggeration and concentration. Backdrops and stage props are kept to a minimum: often a table and two chairs in front of a big curtain. The performers use gestures and body language to represent actions such as opening and closing a door, going up or down a building or a mountain, and embarking, disembarking or traveling by boat. A decorated whip represents a horse, a paddle a boat and two pennants embroidered with wheels a carriage. When an actor walks in a circle, it means that he has gone on a long journey. Four generals and four soldiers represent an army. Two actors can portray groping and fighting in the dark through dance and acrobatics on a brightly-lit stage. By such techniques, Beijing Opera has made it possible to transform a small stage into the whole universe.

With the frequent trips of Beijing Opera troupes abroad, Beijing Opera has won high praise around the world.

Huangmei Opera

Originating in Huangmei County, Hubei Province, Huangmei Opera is a major local opera in Anhui Province. It is a combination of local folk songs, dances and some widely-spread ancient operas. Bordering on Anhui Province, Huangmei in Hubei is a county famous for its tea and tea-picking songs. For this reason Huangmei Opera was originally named "tea-picking tune" or "Huangmei tune." In the old days, rivers often flooded and the homeless victims had to seek refuge in the neighboring provinces. Thus Huangmei Opera was brought to Anhui by victims of flood and famine, where it was greatly enriched and developed to its present form by absorbing the music and performing techniques of Hui Opera and mixing with the local folk songs and dances.

After the founding of the People's Rupublic of China, Huangmei Opera has greatly developed and become a type of "big opera." With the support of the government, Huangmei Opera has bloomed like a wildflower. In particular, the Anhui Provincial Huangmei Opera Troupe's *The Heavenly Maid and the Mortal*(《天仙配》) caused a sensation on the Capital's stage in 1960's and then was made into a film. Huangmei Opera soon spread all over the country.

The opera tells how the Jade Emperor of Heaven has seven daughters, the youngest being the most beautiful Seventh Fairy Maiden. She flees down to the earth and marries

Dong Yong（董永）, an honest, kind-hearted serf, in defiance of her father. She makes the cruel landlord shorten Dong Yong's three year's indenture to 100 days, but just as they are leaving for home, the Jade Emperor finds his daughter's elopement and snatches her back to Heaven, breaking up the happy couple. Pregnant and indignant, she writes a letter in her own blood to Dong, vowing, "When next spring comes and the flowers bloom, I'll return your son beneath the scholar tree（槐树）."

The moving plot, beautiful music and excellent singing made the opera a household word and it traveled abroad to dozens of countries. The success owed much to the excellent performance of the famous Huangmei Opera actress Yan Fengying（严凤英, 1930 A.D.—1968 A.D.）, who made great contributions to the development of Huangmei Opera. With her beautiful voice and superb performing techniques, she created many lovely and true-to-life characters that are still vivid in people's memories. Without her, Huangmei Opera might not have become so popular in China. Now in Anqing city, Anhui Province, a statue of Yan Fengying as Seventh Fairy Maiden has been erected in one of its parks.

Today, besides staging those traditional operas, Huangmei Opera incorporates new developments to reflect modern life. It also experiments with performing famous foreign plays. During the First China's Shakespeare Festival in 1986, audiences both at home and abroad watched with interest an adaptation of Shakespeare's *Much Ado about Nothing* (《无事烦恼》) presented by Anhui Provincial Huangmei Opera Troupe. British Minister Margaret Thatcher sent a message of congratulation to Cao Yu, Chairman of the Chinese Dramatists' Association, saying that Shakespeare would have been greatly amused by the imaginative representation.

Shaoxing Opera

Originating in Sheng County, Zhejiang Province, Shaoxing Opera became a very popular local opera in the eastern part of China at the turn of the nineteenth and twentieth centuries. At that time, the local artists often told stories by singing *changsu diao*（唱书调）, which was the earliest tune of Shaoxing Opera. Influenced by the *yangge*（秧歌）of the

Yuyao area, this singing and story-telling form developed into stage performances around 1909, which were warmly received by the local audience. In a few years, amateur troupes mushroomed in the villages of Sheng County and the nearby regions. The performances were most short plays reflecting the country life, such as *The Selling of the Wife*, *The Bride Comes Back to Her Mother's Home*, etc.

In 1920s, Shaoxing Opera spread gradually to Hangzhou, Haining and some other cities, and to Shanghai by the end of the decade. It was first performed in teahouses or small theatres in Shanghai. By drawing on the tunes of Shao Opera and the dances of Beijing Opera, Shaoxing Opera soon gained the interest of the audience of this metropolis, which was later to become its center. Before 1923, all the actors of Shaoxing Opera were males, and this period of the opera was thus called the "male tune period." After 1923, troupes consisting of only female performers appeared in Shanghai as well as in the countryside of Zhejiang Province. The female troupes developed very quickly and gradually replaced the male troupes. By 1940s, Shaoxing Opera reached its high tide, established in Shanghai and spread to other big cities in East China. It was during this period that some famous Shaoxing Operas were produced, among which *Liang Shanbo and Zhu Yingtai*（《梁山伯与祝英台》）(known to the West as *The Story of Butterflies*), *The Emerald Hairpin*, *Romance in the Western Chamber*, *The Story of the White Snake* and so on were performed again and again even till the present time.

After the founding of the People's Republic of China, great changes and improvement have been made in Shaoxing Opera. It has absorbed the music, dance and performing techniques of other theatrical forms, particularly of *Kunqu* and other dramas. Some new or innovative pieces were created, such as *A Dream of the Red Mansions, Xianglin's Wife*（《祥林嫂》）, etc. At present, Shaoxing Opera is popular not only in East China, but also in many cities in north and central China.

The tunes of Shaoxing Opera are melodious and lyrical. These characteristics make it suitable to represent civil subjects. The most important instrument for music accompaniment is *erhu*（二胡）, while all the other stringed and wind instruments should follow its tune and variations, though in certain cases one of the latter may be played alone for some special effect.

· *Seminar* ·

1. How did Beijing Opera come to its present form?
2. Describe the facial patterns and costumes of Beijing Opera.

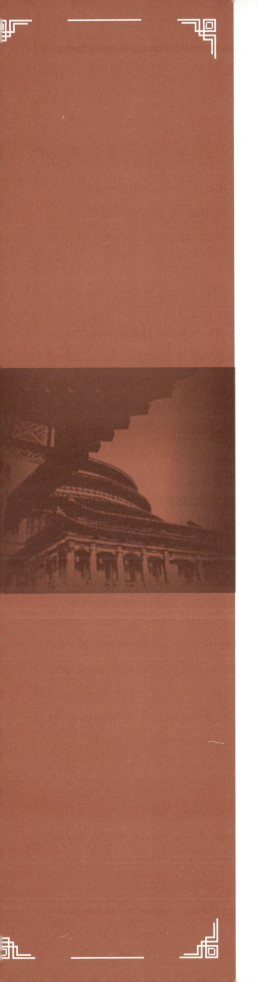

Chapter Four

Science and Technology

- ◆ Four Great Inventions
- ◆ Traditional Chinese Medicine
- ◆ Scientific and Technological Classics

I
Four Great Inventions

Talking of Chinese history, one would not neglect the "Four Great Inventions" which are the great contributions of the Chinese people to the world's civilizations. In this chapter, we'll describe in detail how these "Four Great Inventions" were made in ancient China.

Paper

The earliest Chinese characters were inscribed on bones, tortoise shells and bronze wares in the Shang Dynasty and later, written on silk, bamboo and wood. The earliest Chinese books were made from flat strips of bamboo or wood, inscribed and then threaded together. They were heavy and bulky, inconvenient for reading and carrying. It is said that a man named Dongfang Shuo（东方朔）in the Western Han Dynasty presented a suggestion to the emperor written on 3,000 bamboo strips which had to be carried into the court by two strong men.

Necessity is the mother of invention. Better materials for writing had to be found. In the Eastern Han Dynasty, Cai Lun（蔡伦）, a court eunuch used inexpensive materials such as fibers of tree bark, hemp, rags and old fishing-nets to make paper, known as Cai Lun paper. Light and cheap, it soon became widespread and replaced bamboo or wood strips and silk for writing.

Later on, technological processes and equipment for paper-making were further developed. They were introduced into many foreign countries such as Vietnam, Korea, Japan, India and Arabia, and from Arab countries the techniques spread to Europe and the rest of the world.

The importance of the invention of paper can hardly be exaggerated. It gave a great impetus to cultural progress not only in China but throughout the world.

Printing

The first method of printing in China was the seals—in relief（浮雕）or intaglio（凹雕）. Seals were cut in relief to produce a clear effect—black characters on white paper, but their small size prevented them from printing many characters at a time. Then stone tablets were cut in intaglio, inked and impressions taken off, first on silk and later on paper when it was invented, but the impressions were less clear—white characters on the black background.

Then, in the 6th century block printing（刻版印刷） was invented by combining the two methods used for seals and stone rubbings（摹拓本）. The process of block printing started with the cutting of wood into blocks, and then characters were engraved in relief on the blocks. Ink was brushed on the engraved block and a white sheet of paper spread on it and brushed with a clean brush on its back. The page was printed when the paper was removed.

But the block printing had its drawbacks. It was time-consuming in that blocks had to be engraved each time a new book was printed. It would take several years to finish making the blocks for a thick book.

By the end of the 11th century, a man called Bi Sheng（毕昇） invented movable type printing, which had a far-reaching influence. Bi Sheng first engraved characters on clay dice and put them in fire to turn hard. Then characters were arranged in a frame on an iron plate covered with resin and wax. Being heated, the resin and wax melted. Then another iron plate was used to level the characters to produce type blocks. After a book was printed, the blocks could be dismantled by melting the resin and wax and the characters could be used again. Economical and convenient, the use of these types brought about a revolution in printing.

In the mid-8th century, printing began to be introduced into Korea and Japan in the East and Egypt and Europe in the West, playing a great role in the cultural development of the world.

Gunpowder

The invention of gunpowder was due to the ancient Chinese Taoists' attempt to make "pills of immortality"（长生不老丸） and to turn cheap metals into gold（点石成金）. In their pursuit of impossibilities, the chemists and alchemists（炼丹术士） found that the mixture of saltpeter, sulphur and charcoal powder was explosive. The date of this discovery is unknown since the alchemists liked to operate in secret. The first to record the method of making gunpowder was Sun Simiao（孙思邈）, a well-known pharmacologist of the Tang Dynasty, who also tried to make "pills of immortality."

Gunpowder was not used for rock-blasting and military purposes until the end of the Tang Dynasty. Weapons involving the use of gunpowder, including the cannon, were invented in the 11th century in the Northern and Southern Song Dynasties. In the 13th century, the Yuan troops used various kinds of weapons in the war with the Arab countries in Central Asia, spreading firearms and their manufacture to these countries.

Arab military primers of that time recorded the primitive guns and hand-grenades used by the Mongols.

Gunpowder spread to Europe through the Arabians. During the medieval times, Europeans translated many Arabic books from which they learned about gunpowder. In 1325, the Arabs attacked a Spanish city using a projector to fire "flaming balls" which sounded like thunder. The Westerners became familiar with gunpowder and started studying and manufacturing it. By the 15th century, cannons using gunpowder were being invented by the Europeans.

Compass

The magnetic property of the lodestone (天然磁石) was known to the Chinese as early as the Warring States Period. The primitive compass was invented in the shape of a spoon cut from an intact piece of natural magnetite. The spoon was put in the center of a level tray and rotated. When the spoon stopped, its handle pointed to the south, its head to the north.

Then the Chinese learned to magnetize the iron and invented the "Pointing-to-the-South Fish," a piece of thin iron sheet cut into the shape of a fish, magnetized in a geomagnetic field and put into water, floating and lying north-to-south. Another method was to magnetize a steel needle by rubbing it on a natural magnet. It pointed south when floated on water or suspended. This was the earliest compass.

In the Northern Song Dynasty, the mariner's compass was invented. It was made by putting a magnetic needle on a wooden disk called *luopan* (罗盘). In the Southern Song Dynasty, the *luopan* compass was widely used on merchant vessels plying between China and the Malay Archipelago or India.

The use of the *luopan* compass overcame many difficulties connected with navigation on the high seas. Before the compass was invented, people had to determine direction by the position of the sun in day-time and the stars at night. When it was cloudy and rainy, this had become impossible. The problem remained unsolved until the invention of the compass.

In the early Ming Dynasty, Zheng He (郑和), the navigator and a eunuch of the Ming court, made seven voyages going as far as the east coast of Africa. For each voyage, he brought with him a fleet of 100-200 boats. The compass played an important role in the long distance voyages in ancient China.

The Arabic people learned to use the compass from trading with China, and through the Arabians the compass spread to Europe in the 13th century. From the end of the 15th century to the beginning of the 16th century, European navigators opened many new routes and discovered the American Continent and succeeded in round-the-globe voyages—great events that would not have been possible without the invention of the compass. To some degree, the invention of the compass has brought about economic and cultural exchanges between various countries of the world.

II
Traditional Chinese Medicine

Traditional Chinese Medicine (TCM 中医) is an integral part of Chinese culture. It has a long history and has been sustained by research into every aspect of its use. For thousands of years, it has played an important part in curing diseases and protecting health of the Chinese people, thus contributing greatly to the growth and prosperity of China.

TCM is based on its own theories and contains a unique system of its own. It holds that man and his environment form an organic whole; many diseases are linked with the environment. It also holds that the various parts of the human body form an organic whole. When one is ill, the whole body is affected, so treatment should emphasize the physical condition of the individual as a whole.

TCM, with its unique diagnostic methods, systematic approach, abundant historical literature and materials, is still widely used in treating diseases. It is a medical science which includes theories, hierology (圣学), acupuncture, cupping, massage, *Qigong*, ect.

The Theory of TCM
The basic theory of TCM attempts to explain the nature of life cycle and disease changes. It includes five theories: *Yin* and *Yang*, the five elements (五行), how to direct one's strength, *zangfu* (internal body organs 脏腑) and channels (经络). It also researches dialectics, and explains why diseases occur, how to diagnose and prevent diseases, and how to keep the body in health.

Yin-Yang (阴阳)
The concept of *Yin* and *Yang* comes from an ancient philosophical concept. After observing the natural phenomena, the ancient Chinese grouped all the conflicting ideas into *Yin* and *Yang*. They used this concept to explain how things changed. Chinese medicine used *Yin* and *Yang* to illustrate relationship between various things, such as the different parts of the human body and living things versus nature or society. It is believed

that the relative balance of *Yin* and *Yang* served as the basis to maintain the normal activities of the human body. If such a balance was disturbed, diseases occurred, thus affecting people's health. Because the law of *Yin-Yang* can be applied to anything in existence, it is a very powerful tool of analysis and understanding.

There are five points of the law of *Yin-Yang*:

1）Opposition: Everything has two opposite aspects, *Yin* and *Yang* which struggle with each other and try to control each other.

2）Interdependence: *Yin* and *Yang* define each other and therefore one cannot exist without the other.

3）Mutual consumption and support: *Yin* and *Yang* give off themselves to nourish the other.

4）Inter-transformation: *Yin* can become *Yang*, and *Yang* can become *Yin*.

5）Infinite sub-divisibility: There is always a bit of one in the other.

The Five Elements（五行）

The five elements—wood, water, fire, metal, and earth—emerged from the observation of the various groups of dynamic processes, functions, and characteristics in the natural world. Each of the elements is seen as having a series of correspondences relating both to the natural world and the human body.

TCM uses a system of inter-relationships between the five elements to understand how the various processes of the body support and control each other. Because of these inter-relationships, when one of the organs and its associated element is out of balance, the other elements are also affected. This imbalance will manifest in the individual with different signs and symptoms. It may show in the facial color, the sound of the voice, or a change in the emotional state as well as disharmony in the functioning of the connected organs.

There are two main cycles involved in the five elements: *Sheng*（生）and *Ke*（克）. The *Sheng* Cycle（相生链）is more *Yang*, expensive, oriented with an emphysis on growth and so generating. The *Ke* Cycle（相克链）is more *Yin*, contractive, oriented with an emphysis on control and so restraining.

The *Sheng*/Generating Cycle: The clockwise sequence on the cycle represents the *Sheng* Cycle. Each Element is the mother of the next: metal produces water; water nourishes wood; wood fuels fire; fire makes earth; earth yields metal（金生水，水生木，木生火，火生土，土生金）.

The *Ke*/Regulating Cycle: The clockwise sequence produced by the pentagon represents the regulating or destructive cycle: metal can cut wood; wood can contain earth; earth can absorb water; water can extinguish fire, fire can melt metal（金克木，木克土，土克水，水克火，火克金）.

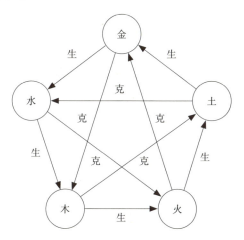

The concepts of *Yin-Yang* and the five elements provide the intellectual framework of much of Chinese scientific thinking in the field of medicine. The organs of the body are seen to be inter-related in the same sorts of ways as other natural phenomina, and best understood by looking for correlations and correspondences.

The Diagnosis of TCM（中医的诊断）

To treat diseases, doctors use the methods of observation（望）, auscultation and olfaction（闻）, interrogation（问）, and pulse feeling and palpation（切）. These methods, known as the four major methods, have their distinctive function each and doctors can make a correct analysis of diseases by applying all of them.

Observation（望）

It is believed that outer appearance is closely linked with the internal organs. If there is something wrong with the internal organs, such changes will be reflected in his/her expressions and appearance. Therefore, doctors can analyze the changes of internal organs by observing the outer appearance.

Auscultation and Olfaction（闻）

By the methods of auscultation and olfaction, doctors try to diagnose diseases by listening to the sound of the patient and smelling the odor of excreta released by the human body. By listening to the sound of the patient, doctor can detect not only the changes of the organs related with sound, but also the changes of the other internal organs. The sounds include: speech sound, breathing, coughing, hawking (clearing the throat noisily), and belching. Also, doctors can smell the odor released by the patient. It is believed that when viruses attack the human body, internal organs and bloods will be affected, thus making body fluid and excreta release a bad smell.

Interrogation（问）

By interrogation, doctors will talk to the patient or someone who knows about the disease (to get information about how the disease occurs, how it develops, its current symptoms, and how it is treated). This method is useful when there no obvious symptoms from the patient outer appearance are available. In this case, interrogation will help the doctors to get the information they need. Also, by interrogating, doctors can obtain other indirect information related with the disease, such as the patient daily life, working environment, food preference, and marital status.

Pulse Feeling and Palpation（切）

Doctors use the method of pulse feeling and palpation by touching and pressing the patients' pulse. It is believed that changes inside the body are reflected by the changes of the pulse activity. Sometimes doctors press the skin of a certain part of the body to identify the nature and the severity of the disease inside the body part.

Methods of Treatment of TCM

Acupuncture（针灸）

According to theory of TCM, there exists a web of pathways called channels（经络）in human body, which link all parts of the body and more than 360 acupuncture points（穴位） are located at these channels. *Qi*, or vitality, flows through these channels and pass these points to support tissues, muscles and organs. When *Qi* is blocked at critical points, the function of issues, muscles and organs will be weakened. So an acupuncturist inserts acupuncture needles at these points to help *Qi* flow, correct *Qi* imbalance, and raise the level of internal energy.

Patients have different sensation towards the treatment of acupuncture. They may feel sore, numb, warm and smelling; but many say that they feel relaxed when the needle is inserted beneath the skin. Many doctors generally use 6 to 8 needles during treatment most of the times but they may use 10 or more needles if two or more symptoms need acupuncture treatment at the same time.

Generally speaking, each treatment takes 20 to 30 minutes, but this relies on the sensitivity and condition of the patient. In short, the success of a treatment depends on the experience and skill of the acupuncturist, on a correct diagnosis of symptoms, accuracy in hitting acupuncture points, timing, depth and angle of insertion and so on.

Moxibustion（艾灸）

Moxibustion is the application of heat to specific points or areas on the body. A smoldering roll or small cone of dried and compacted herbs usually provides the heat source. A smoldering cone of moxa（艾） is placed on a particular acupuncture point to increase the amount of *Yang* in the body. Moxibustion may be used by itself, but is most commonly used as an auxiliary to acupuncture for chronic diseases.

Cupping（拔罐）

The cupping therapy constitutes a significant component part of TCM, and has enjoyed a time-honored history in China. Cupping uses glass cups（sometimes other types of cups are used） to suck the skin. The cup is warmed with a flame then placed on the skin. As the air in the cup cools, the cup sucks the skin. This is rather like massage, except that the skin is pulled rather than pushed.

It is more effective than massage as it helps draw out toxins from the skin.

Massage（*Tui Na* 推拿）

Massage（*Tui Na* in Chinese） means to manipulate the channels of the human body, thus releasing tightness in tissues, stimulating specific points or areas, and facilitating the flow of *Qi*.

Guided by Chinese medicine theory and dialectical principles, a massage is able to cure diseases without the need to take pills or herbal medicine. It is easy to perform and does not have side effects. It can be applied to cure many diseases.

Standard manipulation and special skills are needed to do a massage. The strength used should be persistent, strong, well distributed, mild, deep, and thorough. The hand is most often used for a massage, but the foot, a forearm elbow, and special tools can also be used. Sometimes doctors apply some substances on the body, such as ointment, milk-like liquid, wintergreen, safflower oil, sesame oil, talcum powder, or other lubrication oil.

Gua Sha (刮痧)

The treatment is conducted like this: the skin on the back , limbs, and other parts of the body is lubricated and then pressured and scraped with a rounded object (a ceramic spoon, a piece of jade, or similar object). The method produces "*sha*" which are small red petechiae (瘀斑). *Gua sha* can be used to prevent and treat diseases and strengthen the body. Raising *sha* removes blood stagnation, promoting normal circulation and metabolic processes. It has a very quick effect on pain and an obvious effect on various diseases caused by functional disharmony of the internal organs.

Diet Therapy or Food Therapy (食疗)

The medicinal dishes made by the combination of foods and herbs to treat sickness are food therapy. It is the product of accumulated experience from generation to generation of close monitoring and refinement of recipe. Each recipe is tried-and-true and the natures, characteristics, therapeutic effects and impacts on people are fully known. Besides, most recipes are very delicious and they are specialties in the Chinese cuisine. Food therapy is believed to help improve health on a regular basis, prevent seasonal climate-related problems, fight early symptoms of health problems, complement the primary treatment to combat adverse side effects of harsh drugs during sickness, revive and regain vitality after sickness and repair damages and body malfunctions to restore health.

Herbal Medicine (中草药)

Traditional Chinese herbal medicine is an alternative system of treatment arising from a holistic philosophy of life. It emphasizes the interconnection of the mental, emotional, and physical components within each person, and the importance of harmony between individuals and their social groups, as well as between humanity as a whole and nature. Traditional Chinese herbal medicine is the oldest continuous surviving tradition of herbal medicine in the world.

In Li Shizhen's *Compendium of Materia Medica* (李时珍:《本草纲目》), China's most complete and comprehensive medical book, there list 1892 herbs and 11096 prescriptions. Herbal medicine still plays a very important role in today's medical treatment in China, and the combination of Western medicine and traditional Chinese herbal medicine is preferred by many doctors and patients.

Nowadays, using the advanced scientific techniques to extract the effective substance from herbs has been a focus of the development of traditional Chinese medicine. Tu Youyou（屠呦呦）, together with her research group studied many ancient works on Chinese medicine and prescriptions and found artemisinin（青蒿素） in 1972, which is most effective against Plasmodium falciparum malaria（镰状疟原虫疟疾） and saved the lives of millions of the African people. She was awarded the 2015 Nobel Prize in Medicine for her discovery.

III

Scientific and Technological Classics

Art of War（《孙子兵法》）

Known as "No.1 martial classic of the East," the *Art of War* is also called *Su Zi* or *Sun Wu*. Historical records indicate that *Sun Wu* authored the book during the Spring and Autumn Period. *Sun Wu*, styled Changqing, was a famous strategist living in the State of Qi around the end of the 6th century and the beginning of the 5th century B.C.E. The dates of his birth and death are unknown.

The *Art of War* comprises 13 chapters, with the first 6 dealing with strategies of war and the last 7 focusing on tactics.

Chapter I, "Plans," illustrates the importance of study and deliberation on war, probing into the prerequisites of winning a war.

Chapter II, "On Waging War," analyses the interdependent relation between the war and the people, supplies and finance, emphasizing on quick battles.

In Chapter III, "Attack by Strategy," Sun Zi advocates the strategy of "breaking the enemy's resistance without fighting" and draws the conclusion that "If you know the enemy and yourself, you can fight a hundred battles without perils."

In Chapter IV, "Tactical Dispositions," Sun Zi states that a skillful fighter puts himself into a position that makes a defeat impossible, and conquers the enemy by overwhelming strength.

Chapter V, "Energy," is concerned with creating and utilized of favorable conditions to defeat the rival by a surprising move.

Chapter VI, "Weak and Strong Points," is about how to handle the change of weak and strong points in military operations. Sun Zi notes that "the clever fighter should strike what is weak, avoiding what is strong."

In Chapter VII, "Maneuvering," Sun Zi focuses on the importance of taking up the preferable position and on the prerequisites in military operations.

Chapter Ⅷ, "Variation of Tactics," is on the employment of flexible strategies and tactics.

In Chapter Ⅸ, "The Army on the March," Sun Zi lists the principles of troop marching and encamping.

In Chapter Ⅹ, "Terrain," Sun Zi sums up six kinds of terrain for attacking and withdrawing.

In Chapter Ⅺ, "Nine Varieties of Ground," Sun Zi details the art of war on nine varieties of ground.

Chapter Ⅻ, "Attack by Fire," narrates various kinds of fire attack, their prerequisites and relative methods.

Chapter XⅢ, "Espionage," deals with the roles and ways of using spies and the importance of anti-espionage.

The *Art of War* sums up military tactics during and before the Spring and Autumn Period in ancient China. It is of great significance to both the development of military theory and the promotion of the Chinese philosophy. The influence of the book has reached far beyond the scope of military affairs to cover economy, commerce, education and physical science. In Western countries, many economic theorists have proposed that The *Art of War* be introduced into the sectors of economy and commerce. Now, the book is available in English, Japanese, Russian, German, French and Czech.

Nine—Chapter Arithmetic (《九章算术》)

The *Nine-Chapter Arithmetic* sums up the development of mathematics during the 300 years from the Warring States Period to the Qin Dynasty and is the earliest mathematical work in China.

The *Nine-Chapter Arithmetic* consists of 246 drills that fall into nine varieties. Drills of the same variety are grouped under one chapter. Hence the name the *Nine-Chapter Arithmetic*. The first chapter "Surveying of Land" (方田) deals with the calculation of the land area. The second chapter "Millet" (粟米) details the conversion between all kinds of cereals. The third chapter "Distribution by Progressions" (衰分) dwells upon the problems of distribution among people from different ranks of life, which is equal to the proportional distribution today. The fourth chapter "Evolution" (小广) is about the problems of extraction of a square or cube root. The fifth chapter "Consultation on Engineering Works" (商功) deals with the calculating problems of civil engineering. The sixth chapter "Uniform Transportation" (均输) is about the problems of transportation and forced labor. The seventh chapter "Excess and Deficiency" (盈不足) is about the trade of buying and selling. The eighth chapter "Equation"（方程）is about the solutions to linear equations. The ninth chapter "Legs of a Triangle"（勾股）is about the Pythagorean Theorem（勾股定理）and the problems of measurement.

In an indirect way, the arithmetic drills in the book reflect the economy, politics, and the life of the people of the time. Also, they indicate that the fast developing agricultural production, transportation industry and military operations of the time were presenting demands for mathematics, which in turn helped promote the development of science. Over the course of several hundred years, these drills emerged out of the people's practice and served as teaching materials of "applied mathematics."

Yellow Emperor's Internal Classic（《黄帝内经》）

The *Yellow Emperor's Internal Classic*, or *Internal Classic* for short, whose author is unknown, is the earliest medical classic in China.

Internal Classic includes two parts: *Plain Questions*（《素问》）and *Acupuncture Classic*（《针经》）(or *Miraculous Pivot*《灵枢》), each of which comprises 9 volumes. The 18 volumes originally consist of 162 articles, even though some of the chapters have been lost with the lapse of time.

In a question-and-answer format, *Plain Questions* recounts the discussion between the Yellow Emperor and his royal physician Qi Bo（岐伯）. It mainly sets forth the basic theories of physiology and pathology of the human body. *Acupuncture Classic* dwells upon acupuncture（针灸）and moxibustion（艾灸）, main and collateral channels（经络）as well as hygiene and health care.

Internal Classic lays the foundation for the theoretical systems of traditional Chinese medicine, which has long guided the clinical practice of Chinese medicine and played an important role in China's medical history. It has great significance both inside and outside China. Parts of the book have been translated into Japanese, English, German and French. Many treatises on *Internal Classic* have been published in Japan.

Annotations on Book of Watercourses（《水经注》）

Written by Li Daoyuan（郦道元，472 A.D.—527 A.D.）in the Wei Dynasty, *Annotations on Book of Watercourses* is a famous book on both geography and literature.

Sang Qin（桑钦，?—?）in the Western Han Dynasty is believed to have authored *Book of Watercourses*, which recorded 137 river courses, with introductions to the counties along the banks. But the records were too simple and unsystematic. Taking the form of annotations and with river courses as the guideline, Li made additions to and corrected mistakes in *Book of Watercourses*.

Li's *Annotations* is a 40-volume book, with around 300,000 words, 20 times the length of *Book of Watercourses*. Drawing on more than 400 documents and based on his own field findings, the author recorded 1,252 watercourses, with detailed accounts of the history, customs and landscape along the river banks. In respect of science, Li's *Annotations* is an important reference for geographic research, urban planning, water conservation engineering, and archaeological undertakings in later generations.

In addition, Li's *Annotations* is characterized by vivid description of landscape and places of historic interest. His style exerted a great influence on writers in the Tang and Song Dynasties. Li's *Annotations* is now revered as one of the three most important annotated works in China.

Important Arts for Agriculture（《齐民要术》）

Written by the famous agricultural scientist Jia Sixie（贾思勰，？—？）in the North Wei Dynasty, *Important Arts for Agriculture* is the first complete and systematic book on agriculture in the history of mankind.

The book consists of 92 chapters in 10 volumes, dwelling upon cultivating techniques for various crops, vegetables, fruits, bamboo and trees, livestock and poultry raising, farm produce processing as well as sideline productions. As an agricultural treatise compiled out of ancient documents and field findings, *Important Arts for Agriculture* teems with original ideas and laws for farming. Much of the book is about farming techniques in the middle and lower reaches of the Yellow River, such as arid land preparation, cereals cultivation, grafting from pear trees, sapling breeding, castration for faster growth of livestock and poultry, and so on.

Important Arts for Agriculture attaches great importance to the selection and storage of seeds. For grains alone, the book records 80 species of millets and 24 varieties of rice.

Important Arts for Agriculture presents a systematic summary of farming techniques before the 6th century. It helped boost the advancement of farming technologies not only in the North Wei Dynasty but also in later centuries.

Sketches in Mengxi Garden (Notes Written in Dream)（《梦溪笔谈》）

Written by Shen Kuo（沈括，1031 A.D.—1095 A.D.）in the Northern Song Dynasty, *Sketches in Mengxi Garden* marks a high level of development of ancient China's production and technologies by the Northern Song Dynasty, a level that led the contemporary world.

Shen Kuo, styled Cunzhong(字存中), was a native of Qiantang(钱塘, in today's Hangzhou, Zhejiang). Diligent and industrious from childhood, he acquired the title of *Jinshi*(进士) at the age of 33 and was appointed varied official posts, such as editor in the Zhaowen Imperial Library(昭文馆) and academician(学士) at the Imperial Academy (翰林院). He retreated from politics and settled down in Mengxi Garden in his old age, where he spent years summing up his experiences and research findings and compiling the world famous work *Sketches in Mengxi Garden*.

The book consists of 609 articles bound in 30 volumes, including the three-volume *Addendum to Sketches in Mengxi Garden*(《补笔谈》) and the one-volume *Sequil to Sketches of Mengxi Garden*(《续笔谈》). The writer devotes around one third of its space to recording findings of natural sciences in ancient China, especially those in the Northern Song Dynasty. Its contents cover astronomy, calendar, meteorology, mathematics, geography, geology, mapping, physics, chemistry, biology, medicine, civil engineering, metallurgy and other aspects of science and technology. Many of them are the findings of Shen Kuo's own pains-taking and fully committed research.

Shen Kuo was a great scientist in ancient China and the world. His *Sketches in Mengxi Garden* is a masterpiece of science. Speaking of the book, the famous British historian of science Joseph Lee(李约瑟) once said *Sketches in Mengxi Garden* is "a landmark in China's history of science."

Compendium of Materia Medica(*Ben Cao Gang Mu*)(《本草纲目》)

The author Li Shizhen(李时珍, 1518 A.D.—1593 A.D.), styled Dongbi(字东璧) and assuming the title of the Hermit of Binhu(濒湖山人) in his old age, was a native of Qizhou(蕲州)(in today's Qichun County, Hubei Province). Li was born into a family of doctors, with both his grandfather and father in practice. He took to medicine at an early age. At 14, he acquired the title of *Xiucai*(秀才) but he failed three times in a higher examination. As a result, he gave up efforts to seek after fame and wealth through civil service examinations(科举考试) and fully committed himself to materia medica. Years of painstaking efforts paid off along with his improved medical skills and increasing reputation. For a time, he was recommended to work in the house of King Chu(楚王府) and then the imperial hospital(太医院). Making full use of the facilities there, Li was able to browse through books of medicine, materia medica, and other fields of the past, thus laying a solid foundation for his future efforts to compile *Compendium of Materia Medica*.

Recorded in the 1.9-million-words, 52-chapters, and 16-volumes are 1,897 varieties of medicines grouped under 60 categories. All the recorded medicines were in actual application and had proved effective by the author's time. Besides Chinese herbal medicines, they include animals and minerals for medication. In addition, the book contains 11, 096 prescriptions and 1,160 illustrations. Such enormous contents enable the book to be the greatest treatise of materia medica in history.

Compendium of Materia Medica is more than a masterpiece of pharmaceutics, as it has also contributed to the human knowledge of biology, mineralogy and chemistry.

Compendium of Materia Medica spread to Japan in 1606, then to Korea and Vietnam, and later to Europe around the 16th and 17th centuries. The book is now available either in whole or in excerpts in Latin, French, German, English, Russian and other languages. The world famous scientist Charles Darwin once consulted the book for historical data on the formation of skin colors of gold fish to demonstrate the artificial selection process of animals and gave high comments on it.

A Complete Book for Agriculture（《农政全书》）

Written by Xu Guangqi（徐光启，1562 A.D.—1633 A.D.），a renowned scientist in the Ming Dynasty, *A Complete Book for Agriculture* is the most important book on agricultural science and technology in ancient China.

Xu Guangqi, styled Zixian（字子先） and entitled Xuanhu（号玄扈），was a native of Shanghai County（in today's Shanghai）. He was engaged in farming in his early years. In 1604, he acquired the title of *Jinshi* and thus began his political career, serving as Minister of Rites（礼部尚书） in 1632 while holding the concurrent post of *Dongge Da Xueshi*（东阁大学士），and then *Wenyuange Da Xueshi*（文渊阁大学士） the next year. Xu had extensive research interests while making his greatest achievements in agriculture, astronomy and mathematics. He had close contact with Matteo Ricci（利玛窦，1552 A.D.—1610 A.D.），a Christian missionary, and the two used to work together on their research efforts in astronomy, calendar, mathematics, geography and water conservation. Together, they translated into Chinese many Western books on science. Therefore, Xu was one of the forerunners of introducing Western science into China.

A Complete Book for Agriculture consists of 60 chapters, all together 600,000 words. Its contents generally fall into 12 categories, namely, the science of agriculture, land system, farming techniques, water conservation, farming instruments, crop cultivation, silkworm breeding, plant fabrics, plant cultivation, animal husbandry, manufacturing, as well as disaster reduction and relief. Among them, water conservation and disaster relief take up most of the space. The book collects a large quantity of the ancient and contemporary documents while incorporating the author's own comments. As a masterpiece of agricultural science written by the end of the Ming Dynasty, *A Complete Book for Agriculture* has given a great impetus to the development of agricultural science and technology in China.

Work of Nature and Exploitation of Things (*Creations of Heaven and Human Labor, Works on the Nature's Endowments*) (《天工开物》)

Compiled by Song Yingxing (宋应星, 1587 A.D.—?), a great scientist by the end of the Ming Dynasty, *Work of Nature and Exploitation of Things* is an important document in China's history of science and technology.

The author Song Yingxing, styled Changgeng (字长庚), a native of Fengxin County (奉新县), Jiangxi Province, was born at the end of the Ming Dynasty and died at the beginning of the Qing Dynasty (exact year unknown). He was brought up in an impoverished feudal bureaucratic family. In 1615, the 43rd year of Wanli (万历) (title of a Ming emperor), he passed the imperial examinations at the provincial level, and in 1634 when he was 47, Song was put in charge of education in Fenyi County (分宜县教谕), Jiangxi Province. Then he was transferred to be a justifier (推官) in Jiangzhou County, Fujian Province and later, magistrate of Bozhou County (亳州知县), Anhui Province. *Work of Nature and Exploitation of Things* was completed during his office in Fenyi County.

The 18-volume book records and sums up the remarkable achievements of agricultural and industrial production in ancient China. These include the techniques and organization of crop cultivation, silkworm breeding, silk reeling, spinning and weaving, printing, food processing, salt evaporating, sugar refining, pottery making, metals smelting, casting, forging, welding, and coal mining, as well as the manufacturing of sulfur and lime, paper making, oil extracting, cinnabar making, the making of vehicles, ships and weapons, the collecting and processing of pearl and jade, and so on.

Work of Nature and Exploitation of Things is a vividly illustrated scientific document. The more than 120 illustrations in the book detail the structures and names of tools, production processes and scenes of production, all working to enable the reader to envision the actual situation of that age. The book, with comprehensive knowledge and detailed accounts, has been the pick of books on science and technology at home and abroad. The book was introduced abroad as early as 200 years ago and is now available in Japanese, English and French.

· *Seminar* ·

1. What are the Four Great Inventions in ancient China?

2. How the gunpowder was invented?

3. Describe one of the scientific and technological classics in China.

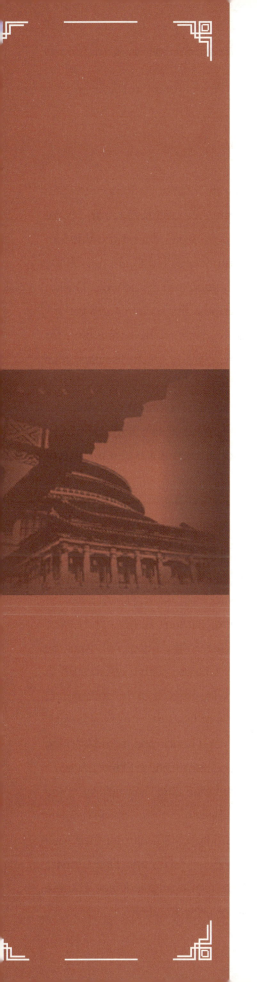

Chapter Five

Education

◆ Ancient Private School
◆ Present Educational System

I
Ancient Private School

Before 1905, there were two kinds of schools in China: the official institutions（官学）, which were open to children of the nobles, and the private schools（私塾）, run by the local scholars, teaching students at home. The official schools began during the Western Zhou Dynasty, and were sponsored by the official constitution called *Guanxue*（官学, official institution）. Only the children of the nobles were admitted into the schools. During the Spring and Autumn, as well as the Warring States Periods, the social contradictions became intense and there appeared hundreds of schools of philosophy contending for their theoretical position. As a result, the states allowed scholars to teach disciples, thus the private schools became popular. Great scholars such as Confucius, Mencious, Mo Zi and Han Fei all enrolled students. Take Confucius for example, he had three thousand students. Among them seventy were virtuous talents. This kind of learning was called *Sixue*（私学, private school）, in contrast to the official kind, constituting an important part of school education in feudal China.

This educational system remained almost unchanged for 2,000 years in China. The aim of education was to train students for the civil service examination（科举考试） in which scholars were selected to be officials at various levels of the bureaucracy. At the court exam, the champion, called *zhuangyuan*（状元）, would be granted a high-ranking position in the court, and sometimes, would even have the honor of being the bridegroom of the emperor's daughter. The second winner was called *bangyan*（榜眼）, and the third, *tanhua*（探花）. They were also assigned important posts in the government. Even the last on the honor roll would be magistrate of a county. The continuation and development of Chinese culture owes much to the civil service examination which guaranteed the officials at various levels of the government a solid basis of education or great learning. But the side effects of this system were apparent. They drove the intellectuals in feudal China to seek after riches and honor, and regard learning as an only means to break away from productive labor and social practice. Many tragedies arose from this educational system. Some of the scholars went mad after their failures in the exam. After their success in the exam, they became rich and honored. Some of the scholars betrayed and deserted their wives who were a great help in time of difficulty on their road to success. Since proficiency in ancient classics such as the *Four Books* and *Five Classics* was required of every candidate in the examination, children from a very early age in these private schools had to recite all those books without interest or understanding.

In 1905, an edict was issued to abolish the civil service examination and the educational system of the past 2,000 years in feudal China came to an end. This dramatic change was brought about by the harsh realities of the country's repeated setbacks and humiliation from the Western powers and the coming of Western missionaries who set up missionary schools to teach science and practical courses.

In place of the old ones, there appeared a new kind of school called *xinxue*（新学, new learning）i.e. public schools which were founded in all parts of the country in which western subjects of study were offered as part of the curriculum, modeled after Western countries. After the Revolution of 1911, China began to develop a Western educational system encompassing all levels of education from primary school to university.

· *Seminar* ·

Comment on the civil service examination: its advantages and disadvantages.

II
Present Educational System

After the founding of the People's Republic of China in 1949, great changes have taken place in China's educational system which has witnessed, especially in recent years, an unprecedented prosperity in the country's educational history. The following is a brief account of the present state of the educational system in China:

Pre–School Education

The main form of China's pre-school education is kindergarten.

Kindergartens enroll children from age two or three to five. With recreational activities occupying the major part of the children's daily life, the kindergarten also offers a curriculum composed of physical education, moral education, language skills, music and art. In some kindergartens in the city or attached to university, English is taught.

Kindergartens are generally staffed with teachers, nurses and doctors. In China, kindergartens may be run by the state, local government, factories, colleges, farms, neighborhood communities, or even by some private homes in recent years.

Nine–Year Compulsory Education

China's Nine-year Compulsory Education is composed of two parts: six-year primary school and three-year junior high school.

Children enter primary school at the age of six. They study in school five days a week. Usually, there are four 40-minute classes in the morning and two in the afternoon followed by outdoor activities. Textbooks are mainly compiled by the State Education Ministry, complemented by some local study materials. Each academic year is divided into two semesters. The first semester is from the beginning of September to late January and the second from the beginning of March to late June. Each year students have two months for summer vacation and one month for winter vacation.

The curriculum of Nine-year Compulsory Education（2001） is shown in the following chart:

Curriculum of Nine-year Compulsory Education（2001）
［九年义务教育课程设置表（2001 年）］

Grade（年级）	一	二	三	四	五	六	七	八	九
Course（课程门类）	Morals and Life（品德与生活）		Morals and Society（品德与社会）				Ideology and Morals（思想品德）		
							History and Society（Or History and Geography）历史与社会（或选择历史与地理）		
			Science（科学）				Science（Biology/Physics/Chemistry）科学（或选择生物、物理、化学）		
	Chinese（语文）	Chinese（语文）	Chinese（语文）	Chinese（语文）	Chinese（语文）	Chinese（语文）	Chinese（语文）	Chinese（语文）	Chinese（语文）
	Math（数学）	Math（数学）	Math（数学）	Math（数学）	Math（数学）	Math（数学）	Math（数学）	Math（数学）	Math（数学）
			Foreign Languages（外语）						
	Physical Education（体育）						Physical Education and Health（体育与健康）		
	Arts（Music or Fine Arts）艺术（或选择音乐、美术）								
	Practical Skills（综合实践活动）								
	Local Teaching Materials（地方与学校课程）								

The curriculum is designed to ensure an all-round development of the students morally, intellectually, physically and aesthetically, based upon the cognitive laws and the needs of the development of children at different ages. It lays emphasis on the integrity of the course knowledge, social life and the students' experience. For instance, for the first and second-year pupils, the course "Morals and Life" is designed to equip them with high morals at early age and adapt themselves to study life. From the third to the sixth year, the course "Morals and Society" aims at learning about society, for the students' life extends from family to school, then to society. For the students of the third to ninth year, the goal of the course "Science" is to help them to form a scientific approach and to cultivate the scientific spirit. The "Arts" course goes through the nine years of the studying process for the purpose of enriching the students' art experience, raising their aesthetic temperament and interest, cultivating their good taste and the appreciation of the beautiful.

High School and Secondary Vocational School

The three-year high school education is a preparation period for the students to go to colleges and universities. The courses include the Chinese language, mathematics, English, physics, chemistry, physiology, history and geography.

In the second or third year, the courses are usually divided into two groups: humanities and science. The former includes history and geography, and the latter embraces physics, chemistry and physiology. The students can select either group of courses according to their needs and interests, for the national entrance examination for colleges practises a system called 3+X, in which 3 stands for the 3 required courses: the Chinese language, mathematics and English while X represents courses chosen from either humanities or science. Secondary vocational education is at the same level as high school. In recent years, vocational schools have been developing swiftly in all medium-size and large cities throughout the country. Besides the courses offered in high school, vocational schools have featured some professional courses such as cooking, cosmetology, tailoring, tourism, accounting, computers and so on. After finishing the three-year course, students can go directly to their jobs in the related field.

Education in China, however, goes beyond the regular school curriculum. During the summer vacation, courses are offered in arts and crafts, Chinese calligraphy and painting, music, and dance. Summer programs sponsored by private enterprises also offer English conversation or athletic activities such as boating, navigation or other out-doors activities.

Higher Education

More than one thousand universities, colleges and institutes in China offer four-or five-year programs. Students who have earned B. A. or B. S. degree may apply for M. A. or M. S. programs and then three-year Ph. D. programs.

China's institutions of higher learning operate on a centralized enrollment system through the nationwide examinations which are given in June. The tests, sponsored by the

Ministry of Education, fall into two categories: humanities, and science and engineering. In addition to Chinese language, mathematics and English, which are compulsory, candidates of humanities are to take either history or geography while those of science and engineering are to take either physics, or chemistry or physiology. There are some differences about the choice of courses for exam in different proviences. New reform of the exam is about to carry on soon.

The candidates may list the institutions and departments they wish to enter in order of preference after the exams. Enrollment is then determined in the light of examination results and a report of their behavior and moral character supplied by the high schools which they have attended. A health certificate must be also attached to the moral report.

A different point of the Chinese universities and colleges from their Western counterparts is that the students must live on the campus, which forms an important part of university life. Living on campus, besides offering many conveniences, provides an ideal setting for mutual understanding and cooperation between students and their professors, as well as fostering both independence and sociability. One drawback of this system is that enrollment is limited due to a lack of accommodations (住宿).

The system of higher education in China requires that students, except in those institutions where the credit system is adopted, follow a prescribed curriculum and undergo a regular series of examinations. The results of these tests are usually recorded in the percentage system (百分制). The final term is devoted to a graduation thesis or a project based on fieldwork or research. A diploma is granted to students who have completed all the required courses and passed all the exams and a bachelor's degree is conferred on students whose grades exceed the standard plus an assessment by faculty members. Diploma and MA/MS are granted to graduate students in the same manner, but they are required to pass their thesis defence before a committee.

Besides the regular universities and colleges, there are three-year adult vocational schools of higher learning, providing an opportunity for in-service workers to acquire a diploma of higher learning. These forms of school include correspondence (函授), evening school (夜大), TV university (电大) and vocational colleges (高职) and self-taught programs (自学考试).

· *Seminar* ·

1. Comment on the curriculum of the Nine-year Compulsory Education.

2. Describe *Sixue* (私学, private school) in ancient China.

3. Give a description about China's present secondary vocational education and vocational colleges.

Chapter Six

Manners and Customs

◆ China's Tea Culture
◆ China's Wine Culture
◆ China's Culture of Food
◆ Traditional Festivals
◆ Other Traditional Customs

I
China's Tea Culture

Tea-drinking is a constituent part of Chinese culture. China is an original producer of tea and its skills in planting and making tea, its customs of tea-drinking spread over to Europe, and then, to many other regions through cultural exchange via the ancient "Silk Road" and other channels of trade. The Chinese nation has written a brilliant page for its tea culture in the history of world civilization. Together with silk, tea is the pride of the Chinese nation. The development and promotion of tea has been one of China's principal contributions to the world.

According to Lu Yu's *Tea Classics* (陆羽, 733 A.D.—804 A.D.,《茶经》), tea-drinking in China can be traced back to the Zhou Dynasty: "Tea was discovered by Shennong and became popular as a drink in the State of Lu because of Zhou Gong." （茶之为饮，发乎神农氏，闻于鲁周公。） Tea-drinking in China has a history of four thousand years. As the legend has it, Shennong, a legendary hero, tasted hundreds of wild plants to see which were poisonous and which were edible, so as to prevent people from eating the poisonous plants. It is said that he was poisoned seventy-two times in one day but was saved by chewing some tender leaves of an evergreen plant blossoming with white flowers. Since he had a transparent belly, people could see how the food moved throughout his stomach and intestines. When they saw the juice of the tender leaves go up and down in the stomach as if it were searching for something, they called it "查" (*cha*), meaning search. Later it was renamed "茶" (*cha*) having the same sound of "查". In the end, Shennong was poisoned by a kind of small grass with small yellow flowers. He felt great pain in the belly and before he could eat some tea, his intestines broke into pieces and he died. That little grass is called "breaking-intestines grass" (断肠草). People told and retold this story from generation to generation, paying great respect to their ancestor who pioneered agriculture and Chinese medicine.

Tea has been used as one of the sacrificial offerings to gods and ancestors from ancient times in China. In Liu Jingshu's *Fantastic Garden* (刘敬叔, ?—468 A.D.,《异苑》), of the Southern Dynasty, there is an interesting story: A young widow lived with her two sons. They were all fond of drinking tea. But before drinking, the young mother would offer a cup of tea to an ancient tomb in their courtyard. Her two sons became disgusted with this practice and decided to dig up the tomb. But they were stopped by the mother. That night a spirit appeared in that woman's dream saying that "I am a spirit living in the ancient tomb for three hundred years. I am grateful to you for your protection and offering of the fragrant tea. Though I am a heap of rotten bones, I'll surely repay you." The next morning they found in their courtyard one thousand strings of ancient coins with a new thread binding them together. From this story we know it had become a practice to offer tea to god or ancestors at the memorial ceremony.

Tea was also used as a funerary object in ancient times. In an ancient tomb of Western Han Dynasty unearthed at Ma Wang Dui (马王堆) in the suburbs of Changsha, Hunan Province, tea was listed in the brochure of burial articles.

Tea has had close connection with religion in China. In the history of China, tea is usually regarded as a kind of drink that would refresh oneself and make the mind calm. The Buddhists aim at refraining from daily pleasures, and sitting and amusing themselves with Buddha's teachings. Tea is their ideal drink to cultivate their moral character. In Buddhism, tea is praised as a sacred thing given by God. Tea-drinking is a nation-wide custom in China. It is a daily necessity for the Chinese to have three meals and tea a day (一日三餐茶饭). When any guest comes, it is a rite to present a cup of tea to him/her. There are numerous teahouses in every town and city. Often many elderly people rise early in the morning and hurry to the teahouse to enjoy a cup of tea. A teahouse is a society as shown by Lao She's famous play *The Teahouse* (《茶馆》).

Tea-drinking is an art, a learning in China. In some places, the way of making tea is very complicated. And the tea utensils—the teacup, tea saucer, teapot, tea tray—are works of art. *Dianxin* (点心 pastry), which goes with tea, both tasty and appealing, is loved not only by the Chinese but also by the people all over the world. There are hundreds of famous teas in China and there are a great many famous springs and streams to provide water to make tea. Foreigners have found that there are several springs in China named "the First Spring under Heaven" (天下第一泉). Good tea needs good water. And the tea fields or tea mountains are also marvelous sights to add beauty to the scenery.

Literature is a mirror of life. As tea has been closely woven into the life of the Chinese people, so has it been into literature. There are several thousands of classic poems about tea left to us. Bai Juyi, the great poet of Tang Dynasty, was particularly fond of tea. He wrote more than fifty poems about tea. In his famous *Poem of A Pipa Player* there are these lines:

The merchant cared for money much more than for me,

One month ago he went away to purchase tea.

（商人重利轻别离，前月浮梁买茶去。）

Lu You, the great patriotic poet of Southern Song Dynasty, wrote more than three hundred poems in which tea was mentioned.

Tea has entered almost every other form of literature and art—novels, paintings, plays, songs and dances, couplets. In the great novel of Qing Dynasty, *A Dream of the Red Mansions*, there are about three hundred mentions of tea. So people say the novel is permeated with the fragrance of tea（一部《红楼梦》, 满纸茶叶香）. There are thousands of paintings describing tea-drinking affairs and the scenery of tea fields and there are a variety of tea-picking dances among the minority nationalities in China. So we can find these lines frequently quoted:

Wine can add virginity to heroes,

While tea can stir up men of letters to create.

（酒壮英雄胆, 茶引文人思。）

Kinds of Chinese Tea

Chinese tea is famous throughout the world for its unique color, fragrance, flavor and finely shaped leaves. According to the ways of manufacturing, Chinese tea can be divided into six categories: Green Tea, Black Tea, Oolong Tea, White Tea, Scented Tea, and Tea Lumps. However each category can be further divided into numerous subcategories.

Green Tea（绿茶）

Green Tea has the longest history and still ranks first in production and variety in China. People like its freshness and natural fragrance. Green Tea is made by simply but carefully heating the leaves which must be kept green and unbroken while they are being heated. Famous green tea include *Longjing*（龙井）Tea from the West Lake of Hangzhou, *Maofeng*（毛峰）Tea from Huangshan Mountain, *Yinzhen*（银针）Tea from Junshan Mountain, *Yunwu*（云雾）Tea from Lushan Mountain and *Biluochun*（碧螺春）Tea from Jiangsu.

We'll say a few more words about *Longjing*. The *Longjing* Green Tea gets its name from a nearby scenic spot called *Longjing*（Dragon Well）. The tea is featured by four traditional characteristics: its leaves are fresh green in color, fragrant in aroma, full in taste, and smooth and even in appearance. The best tea is picked in early spring on the tea hills. Just as a local saying goes: "Best tea from the hills and best flowers from the plain."

Black Tea（红茶）

Black Tea also enjoys a good reputation both at home and abroad. Different from Green Tea, Black Tea is thoroughly fermented. In the fermentation, the tea leaves turn from green to black.

Oolong Tea（乌龙茶）

Oolong Tea possesses the freshness of green tea and the fragrance of the black. In recent years, it has become popular with more and more people for its effects in helping to reduce high blood pressure, lower the cholesterol, prevent coronary heart disease and aid digestion.

Oolong Tea has been produced in Fujian Province for at least 400 years. Today it is also grown in Guangdong and Taiwan. Because the tea grows on cliffs which people rarely reach, it is difficult to pick. So it is considered the most precious.

White Tea（白茶）

White Tea is as white as silver. The major producing areas are Fujian's Zhenghe and Fuding. Famous varieties include *Yinzhen* (silver needle) Tea and White Peony Tea.

Scented Tea（花茶）

Scented Tea (also called Flower Tea) is a variety unique to China, having the smells of flowers. When put in boiled water, the dried flowers spread as fresh as they were just picked up. Sweet osmanthus, jasmine, rose, orchid and plum flowers can all be used.

Tea Lumps（茶块）

The Black Tea or Green Tea is pressed into the shapes of brick, cake or ball. The Tea Lump is convenient to store and transport and is suitable for minority people in border regions. The major producing areas of tea lumps are in Hunan, Hubei, Sichuan, Yunnan and Guangxi. The most famous tea lump is Yunnan's *Pu'er*（普洱）Tea, which has great therapeutic effects. One recorded example shows that, among 20 patients suffering from high cholesterol, those who drank three cups of this tea every day for one month experienced a 22% drop in their cholesterol levels, but those who drank ordinary tea three times a day showed no change.

The Yunnan Compressed Tea is a suitable beverage for all ages. It is also known as a diet tea and beauty tea as well.

There are some special kinds of tea among the minority people—*Leicha*(Pounded Tea)in Hunan and Oil Tea in Guangxi.

Leicha（擂茶）, also called *sanshengtang*（三生汤）, is popular in Taoyuan County, Hunan Province. It has a history of more than 1, 600 years. As legend has it, during the Three Kingdoms Period, Zhang Fei（张飞）, a general of Shu, led his army into the Wuyi Mountain against his enemy. As his army passed Wutou Village（present-day Taoyuan）, many of his soldiers were ill. It was summer and pestilence was spreading. The general himself was sick. He ordered his army to stop at the village for a rest. Despite their illness, Zhang Fei ordered some of his soldiers to help the villagers harvest their crops and sent others to look for doctors and medicine. An old woman was deeply moved when she saw the army so well-disciplined. She went to the general and gave him the "recipe" for *Leicha*, which had been a secret handed down by her ancestors. After drinking the tea, Zhang Fei and his soldiers recovered quickly. The army marched on and won a great victory. From then on, the tea's fame spread.

The process of making the tea is very complicated and must be followed strictly. First raw ginger, rice, and tea leaves are put in a wooden bowl and pounded into paste with a hawthorn stick whose fragrance will go into the paste. Then the paste is divided among several bowls and boiling water is poured in. Sugar, salt and sometimes, sesame are added to the tea. The tea made in this way has a variety of flavors—hot, salty and sweet. It can stimulate body energy, and is believed to be good for the liver and stomach.

Oil Tea, popular among the Miao and Dong minority nationalities in Guangxi, has a similar procedure of making the *Leicha*. The different point is that the mixture of ginger, rice and tea leaves has to be fried with oil. The local people often entertain their guests with Oil Tea on festivals and holidays. Refreshments, such as cakes, sweet potatoes, peanuts and fried soybeans are often served with the tea.

· *Seminar* ·

1. What is China's earliest tea classics?

2. Tell the story of Shennong.

3. Tell the story of Zhang Fei（张飞）and *sanshengtang*（三生汤）.

4. What's the difference between Green Tea and Black Tea?

Ⅱ
China's Wine Culture

Wine has a close connection with culture in China both in ancient and modern times. In the book *The Spring and Autumn in the Cup*（《杯里春秋》），the author Lin Chao（林超） has written his famous line: "Wine drinking is something of learning rather than eating and drinking."（饮酒者，乃学问之事，非饮食之事也。）

Wine has a history as long as that of mankind. According to legend, the Chinese people began to make wine with grains seven thousand years ago; with animal milk, ten thousand years ago.

Wine permeates into every field of life: law, philosophy, ethics, morality and social customs. In fact a drop of wine can reflect the concepts of religion and law, the relations of ethics and morality, the system of grades of different nations.

Because most emperors and ministers in ancient China were fond of wine, wine became a part of political life, playing an important role of moderation and destruction. According to legend, Emperors Yao and Shun could drink a thousand cups of wine at a time（尧舜千钟），and as historical record goes, Emperor Wu of Han, fond of wine, made a policy for the exclusive right of wine by the state, thus bringing great fortune to the government. The role of wine was played to the full by emperors and ministers in ancient China in winning over people's support and realizing their political aims. The most famous example is the story how Emperor Taizu of Song（宋太祖） deprived a military commander of his command by serving him wine（杯酒释兵权）.

Wine appealed to men of letters and many anecdotes about their drinking were handed down from generation to generation. Li Bai, the most famous poet of the Tang Dynasty, is also called "the sage of wine." About one-sixth of his poems are connected with wine. The most well-known stanzas are as follows:

My fur coat worth a thousand coins of gold.

And my flower-dappled horse may be sold.

To buy good wine that we may drown the woes age-old.

（五花马，千金裘，呼儿将出换美酒，与尔同销万古愁。）

Wine also has close connection with social customs in China. There are fifty-six nationalities in China and drinking customs vary from nationality to nationality. For instance, the Mongolians will present three cups of wine to a guest and go on singing songs of wine until the guest finishes them.

So wine-drinking has permeated into Chinese culture. In a sense, wine is the zymase of Chinese culture.

Alcoholic Beverages in China

Foreign visitors can find hundreds of restaurants and eating-houses in every city of China. On the show window of every restaurant, there is a variety of alcoholic beverages on sale. Indeed, China uses a billion tons of grain in brewing wines each year.

Few countries have a longer history than China for the brewing of alcoholic beverages and much Chinese literature and tradition includes references to the enjoyment of wine. The ancient poets—Li Bai, Du Fu and Wang Wei—all had a deep love for wine.

Chinese wines are classified into the following four groups, according to the process by which they are made:

Huangjiu（黄酒）(*also known as Laojiu*)

Huangjiu, brewed from grain, predates all the other liquors, with a history of several thousand years. The alcohol content is mild, at around 15%, and it is used as the base of *Yaojiu* ("yao" means medicine in Chinese). It is also an excellent condiment for cooking. Among these liquors, the Shaoxing Rice Wine is the most famous.

Baijiu（白酒）

Baijiu includes all spirits, is made from sorghum, corn, barley or wheat, which are easy to ferment. Colorless and transparent, it usually contains over 50% alcohol. A small quantity can make one tipsy in a moment. Of the most famous of *Baijiu* are Guizhou Maotai, Wuliangye, Shanxi Fenjiu and Luzhou Daqu.

Pijiu（啤酒）(*beer*)

Chinese beer has a very short history, yet it has become very popular, and production is booming. Beer is available in barrels and bottles. Qingdao beer is the most famous.

Tianjiu（甜酒）

Grape wine and wines made from other fruit juices, are collectively called *Tianjiu* ("tian" means sweet in Chinese).

Yaojiu is also included in this group, which is made from Chinese herbal medicines mixed into a base of *Huangjiu* or *Baijiu*. Nothing could be more varied than Chinese *Yaojiu*. There are countless types of alcoholic drinks containing secret potions, and species, such as snakes, soft shelled turtle, tiger bones and antler, all of which are associated with Chinese herbal medicine. They have, respectively, health effects in curing some diseases, strengthening the constitution, improving sleep quality and relieving fatigue.

Dozens of wine advertisements appear on the TV every day in China, making an impression that wine-drinking constitutes a part of the virility of man. And there is a saying among the drinkers, "Those who cannot drink wine are no men." As the current custom goes, much business is done and many important problems are settled at the meal table when some cups of wine are drunk.

Some Famous Chinese Wines
Maotai (茅台)

Maotai is regarded as one of the national wines and king of the Chinese spirits. A few cups of Maotai would relieve you from years of sorrow. No banquet in China is complete without toasts on this fiery liquor.

Made in the town of Maotai, Guizhou Province, it has a history of 2,100 years. It was favored by Emperor Wudi of the Western Han Dynasty.

Legend has it that there lived an industrious, honest old man. One piercing winter day, a poor-dressed girl passed by his door. Out of sympathy he invited her into his home and gave her a cup of wine to warm her. At night, the old man dreamt of seeing a fairy arrive at his home, who bore a striking resemblance to the girl. She poured a cup of fairy liquor under the willow tree in front of his house. The following day, the old man found a well under the willow containing fresh and sweet liquor. The drink distilled from that had an unparalleled fragrance. Today the liquor's brand mark still depicts the fairy maiden holding a cup. The two silk ribbons tied around the bottle are derived from the streamers around her waist.

The brewing techniques of Maotai are very complicated. Local quality sorghum and wheat are the raw materials. Cultivating yeast, fermenting and distilling are done at high temperature. Whole and crushed kernels of grain in measured proportions are mixed, then steamed and cooked. Twice during the brewing, the grains are fed into fermenting pools; soaked in spirits, fermented eight times (once a month), and distilled seven times.

The liquor from each distillation is then aged in cellars for at least three years before being blended into Maotai, thus bringing out its characteristic savor with its nutritious food value.

For years, the Maotai flavor has puzzled brewers from other cities. Distilleries in other parts of the country have invited the best distillers from the town of Maotai to be their advisers. The distillers did all they could, but each time the product turned out to be a failure. People say that the secret is a combination of right temperature, a misty climate and the water and soil of the town. The distillation process is especially adapted to the exceptional advantages of the natural environment. It can't be made anywhere else.

In 1915, the U.S. government held an exhibition to celebrate the Panama Canal's opening to navigation. The Chinese government sent a delegation and brought some Maotai liquor to the exhibition. One of the delegates accidentally dropped a bottle of Maotai on to the floor of the exhibition hall. It broke and the fragrant smell filled the hall and attracted all the participants. Maotai won a gold medal. In 1985, it won another gold medal in a competition in France.

Fen Liquor（汾酒）

Produced in the Apricot Blossom Village in Fengyang County, Shanxi Province, Fen Liquor is one of the ten famous Chinese wines in China.

Fen Liquor has a history of more than 1, 500 years. It is traditionally made from fine barley and peas. Fragrant and delicate with a lingering after-taste, it is also used to treat various diseases. The liquor does not settle or get muddy in storage; the longer it is preserved, the better the taste.

Fen Liquor won a grand prize at the Panama International Exhibition in 1915, and it has won dozens of prizes both at home and abroad, including a gold medal issued by the State Council in 1980. Sold in more than 50 countries, it has been savored by tourists from Japan, the United States, New Zealand, Britain and many other countries.

Bamboo-leaf Green Liquor（竹叶青酒）

Bamboo-leaf Green Liquor is made by immersing bamboo leaves and dozens of medicinal herbs, such as Chinese angelica and cap jasmine in Fen Liquor. The wine is pale green, translucent and fragrant. It has a reputation for improving health and treating such diseases as heart trouble, high blood pressure and arthritis. Bamboo-leaf Green Liquor won the State Council's gold medal in 1979 and is now sold throughout the world.

Shaoxing Wine (绍兴酒)

Shaoxing Wine, also called *Laojiu* (老酒, old wine), *Huangjiu* (黄酒, yellow wine), produced in the town of Shaoxing, Zhejiang Province, is one of the best and mildest intoxicants made from gluttonous rice and wheat. Among its varieties, *Jia Fan Huangjiu* (加饭黄酒) is the most famous. It has been known for its flavor and golden color.

Shaoxing Wine has a history of over 2,000 years. Many stories are still told about the wine across the country. In 353 A.D., during the Jin Dynasty, the local county official and famous calligrapher, Wang Xizhi, invited 41 well-known scholars to Lanzhu Hill outside Shaoxing city for religious service. After the ceremony, he asked the guests to take a rest on the banks of a winding stream and had a cup filled with wine float with the current. If the cup stopped or over-turned, the person nearest to it had to compose a poem or drink three cups of wine. Thirty-seven poems were written during the gathering. Drunk but elated, Wang Xizhi wrote a preface for them on a piece of silk with a brush made of mouse whiskers. His running hand writings have been considered to be some of the best ever seen.

Shaoxing Wine won two gold medals in international competitions in 1985—one in Paris, the other in Madrid. Processed at a low temperature using prolonged fermentation, the wine resembles dry sherry and is popular all over China.

Dukang Wine (杜康酒)

Dukang Wine, which has the charms of historical relics and the pureness of nature, bears the same name of its production site—Dukang village in Henan Province. The wine has been popular among the Chinese people for more than 2,500 years. It may not only arouse your deep-seated nostalgia for the ancient past, but also give you a natural enjoyment by relieving your anxiety. Dukang Wine is as good to health as it is to prolonging life.

The unique style of Dukang has won it the eulogy of Jingongxian Wine (进贡仙酒). Cao Cao, a famous general in the Three Kingdoms Period, wrote, "Only Dukang Wine can relieve my anxiety" (何以解忧, 唯有杜康). The well-known poet Du Fu in the Tang Dynasty also wrote, "As Dukang Wine can bring happiness to men, no wonder Zhang Li preferred none other than Dukang Wine" (杜酒频劳劝, 张梨不外求). In 1970s, when a national banquet was hosted by the Chinese Government for the Japanese Prime Minister Kakuei Tanaka (田中角荣), the latter specially mentioned to Premier Zhou Enlai that he preferred Dukang Wine to any others.

· Seminar ·

1. How many kinds can the Chinese alcoholic beverages be grouped into?
2. Tell the origin of Maotai's brand mark.

III
China's Culture of Food

The most thriving enterprise in the world is restauranting. Among the most prosperous are Chinese restaurants.

Chinese food is known for its variety and abundance. According to data on the subject, the number of well-known ancient and modern Chinese dishes amounts to 8,000. The ingredients may be roughly classified into 600 categories. There are 48 different basic ways of cooking, including roasting, frying and boiling, all of which bring out the best of the ingredients. Besides, Chinese cooking lays emphasis on the three essentials: color, flavor and taste, and thus every dish on the Chinese meal table looks like a piece of art, good-looking and delicious.

China is a vast country. Each area has a wealth of local specialities in its cooking. This means that the range of ingredients and cooking styles is incredibly wide and varied. Nevertheless, cooking in China may be grouped into the following four major schools:

Northern School

It includes Beijing, Shandong, Tianjin and Henan cooking, which is also called *Jing Cai*（京菜 , Beijing Dishes）in Chinese.

Most of the *Jing Cai* have a high calorie value answering the demands of the cold northern climate. Well-known Beijing dishes include Whole Roast Duck or "Peking Duck"（北京烤鸭）, *Shuan Yang Rou*（涮羊肉）(slices of lamb which you dip in boiling water and then in a do-it-yourself sauce), roasted lamb and crab.

Peking Duck gourmets are unanimous that this dish is the best in Beijing. The raising of ducks is called *Tianya*（填鸭）(stuffing of ducks). Specially prepared feed is provided at regular intervals so that ducks will gain more flesh and fat. Ducks are roasted whole, cooked over a fire of Chinese palm wood. The ducks are so roasted that the skin becomes crispy and brown and the meat juicy and tender.

Shuan Yang Rou（Mutton Hotpot）is a Mongolian dish. Only small lambs from Inner Mongolia in the north are used. Mutton is sliced wafery thin and is cooked in a pot of boiling water for a very short time. The mutton is then dipped into a delicious sauce including soy sauce, pepper, ginger, red pepper oil, sesame seed oil, sesame seed paste, preserved bean curd and spring onion, and tastes tender and juicy.

Kao Yang Rou (roast lamb) consists of minced mutton mixed with raw eggs, and is cooked on a hot iron plate with preserved clam sauce. Traditionally, one stands while eating this dish.

Sichuan School (in the upper reaches of the Yangtze)

This is the main style in the Sichuan Province and is called *Chuan Cai* (川菜) in Chinese.

Sichuan Province is a mountainous area in Southwest China. The district was developed in ancient times, and extensive water utility works were built 2,000 years ago during the Qin Dynasty. It boasts an excellent traditional culture supported by a mild climate, fertile land and rich resources. The ingredients of its dishes are mainly mountain produce and river fish simply because the region has no sea coast. One of the reasons for its fine cooking could be the fact that skillful chefs were taken to the district by high officials sent by the central government during the Yuan, Ming and Qing periods. Most of these chefs settled in Sichuan and developed new cooking styles based on Beijing cuisine. They used ingredients indigenous to the district and adapted the dishes to local taste.

Sichuan dishes are distinguished for being "spicy and hot." Their uniquely hot, pungent flavor is created by a mixture of spices and condiments, including red pepper, garlic and ginger.

Jiang Zhe School (in the middle and lower reaches of the Yangtze and also the east coast)

This style prevails in Shanghai, Hangzhou, Ningbo and Suzhou, and is also known as the Shanghai School, or *Huai Cai* (淮菜) in Chinese.

The basin of the lower reaches of the Yangtze and the coast are blessed with the produce of rivers, lakes and the sea—everything for seekers of fine food. Shanghai dishes are characterized by the addition of a relatively high proportion of soy sauce. The infinite variety of Shanghai dishes includes such unique local treats as "Yangzhou" and "Ningbo."

Shanghai crab is one of the greatest specialities. Crabs are in season from November through December. The locals claim that Shanghai crabs are not only larger than those of Beijing but are the tastiest in the entire country.

Southern School

This is known as the Canton School or *Yue Cai*（粤菜）in Chinese.

It includes Guangdong, Chaozhou and Guangxi cooking. A lucky person is "to be born in Suzhou; to live in Hangzhou; to be fed in Canton", as a Chinese saying goes.

It is also said that the people of Beijing are lovers of leisure pursuits; the Shanghainese are extravagant in dress; and the Cantonese are gourmets.

Indeed, Guangdong may be said to have a greater variety of food than any other place in the world. There is also a saying among foreign visitors: "The two Guangs （people in Guangdong and Guangxi）eat practically everything that walks on the ground, swims in the water and flies in the air except CAAC."

· Seminar ·

Cooking in China may be grouped into four major schools. Tell the characteristics of each.

IV
Traditional Festivals

In the more than 5,000 years history of China, many festivals have gradually been shaped in the country. The origins of China's traditional festivals can be traced to the Shang and Zhou Dynasties. According to their origins, China's traditional festivals fall roughly into three categories: agricultural, religious and social festivals. These three kinds of festivals infiltrated and influenced one another and gradually blended to form China's festivals today.

According to their contents, Chinese festivals can be divided into five types: agricultural, sacrificial, commemorative, recreational, and celebratory festivals. Agricultural festivals, such as the Beginning of Spring（立春）, the Spring Equinox（春分） and so on, are mainly concerned with farming, forestry, fishing and hunting activities; sacrificial festival, such as the Pure Brightness（清明）, and the Mid-autumn Festival are derived from religious sacrificing days, on which people offer sacrifices to gods, to their ancestors and deceased relatives to pray for protection against evil ghosts and disasters; commemorative festivals are festivals when people commemorate their national heroes; recreational festivals are usually spent with singing, dancing and other recreational activities, of which the song or torch festivals of some minority nationalities are examples; celebration festivals are the main festivals of the country, typical of which is the Spring Festival（春节）, during which people celebrate a bumper harvest and congratulate each other on their good fortune, good health and happiness. Since China is such a big country with a territory of 9.6 million square kilometers and 56 nationalities, some of the festivals are national, some regional, and some, observed only by certain ethnic groups. At present, some national festivals, such as the New Year's Day, May Day, and National Day, are observed in China.

The Spring Festival（春节）

Equal to Christmas of the West in significance, the Spring Festival is the most important holiday in China. It begins on the New Year Day of the lunar calendar and lasts about two weeks.

Two features distinguish it from the other festivals. One is seeing off the old year and ringing in the new. The other is family reunion. Sons and daughters working away from home come back to join their parents.

Two weeks before the festival the whole country is permeated with a holiday atmosphere. Shops and streets are beautifully decorated and every household is busy shopping, preparing for the festival. In the past, all families would make a thorough house-cleaning, settling accounts and clearing off debts, to "pass the year"（过年）. After putting up couplets and pictures on the doors on the Lunar New Year's Eve, the last day of the twelfth moon in the Chinese lunar calendar, each family gathers for a sumptuous meal called "family reunion dinner"（团圆饭）. After the dinner, they sit together before the TV to watch the New Year's Program. About ten minutes before the ringing of the New Year's bell, people let out fireworks and firecrackers to welcome back the Kitchen God from Heaven, who is in charge of the fortune and misfortune of the household he dwells.

On the first three days of the festival, people visit their best friends and close relatives, exchanging greetings and presents, which is known as "New Year's visits"（走亲戚）. The Spring Festival carnivals take place at the same time. There are performances of dragon dance and lion dance and recreational parades in the streets by some recreational troupes.

Some of the customs based on superstitions are quite interesting. For example, on New Year's Day, people will not sweep the floor, do washing or dump their garbage out of the house, lest these would do away with their fortune. On the Lunar New Year's Eve, people like to stick the Chinese character "福" (happiness) upside down on doors or walls, because "upside down" in Chinese is a homophone of "coming" or "arriving." The custom of pasting couplets on doors has a long and interesting history. In ancient times, people hung short pieces of peach trees branches on doors or at front gates for the purpose of driving away evil things. Later they became peach-wood boards with some Chinese characters written on them. With the invention of paper, these peach-wood tablets were replaced by long scripts of red paper, on each of which was written a verse line to welcome the new year or to express wishes for happiness and good fortune. During the long process of history, spring couplets have become a special form of literature with their own characteristics.

On the evening of the 15th day of January, lunar calendar, there is a lantern show in the streets or parks of the city. Lanterns in all shapes, colors and sizes make the place a marvelous sight. With the lantern show over, the Spring Festival comes to an end and people will go back to their work and farmers will be busy with their spring ploughing and sowing.

The Lantern Festival (元宵节)

The Lantern Festival is one of the most traditional and colorful of Chinese holidays. Falling on the 15th day of the first month in Chinese lunar calendar, it is really "a festival within a festival," bringing the Spring Festival to a climax. According to historical records, this festival began to prevail in the Western Han Dynasty and flourished during the Tang and Song Dynasties. Its present name is in fact derived from the Tang custom of hanging out lanterns on the night of the festival.

Lanterns can break darkness, illuminate the land and bring brightness and hope to people. So the Lantern Festival has been observed by people for more than one thousand years and celebrated all over China.

On that night, shops and temples are decorated with colorful lanterns made of paper, gauze and glass, depicting legendary figures, landscapes and birds and flowers. There are also performances of drum dances, dragon lantern dances and stilt walking (高跷) in the streets and lanes. On that day, people eat round dumplings which are made of glutinous rice flour and filled with a variety of sweet fillings, called *yuanxiao* (元宵), that is why the festival is also called *Yuanxiao Jie* (元宵节). The shape of *yuanxiao* is like a ball and the food is eaten on the night of the first full moon of the new year. These two factors combined symbolize the family's reunion, for the Chinese word for "reunion" is *tuanyuan* (团圆). The first Chinese character *tuan* means something shaped like a ball, and the second *yuan* round.

In the old days, the way people celebrated the Lantern Festival varied from place to place. In the north, people made lanterns of ice in the shape of human figures, buildings and fruits with a candle light in them. When all the candles were lit, the lantern show was a marvelous sight. In some cities in the south, with a stream flowing through, people made paper boats floating the lanterns. In Beijing, many worshipers would go to the White Cloud Temple on the eighth day of the first lunar month, where they burnt scents, offered up prayers and sacrifices and donated money, wishing to expel bad luck and disasters in the year ahead. A trade market was held in the capital between the eighth and sixteenth days. People could buy lanterns, flowers, jewels, silk, antiques, toys and many other things there. Beijing's lantern fair usually was held at the north end of Wangfujing Street. In Suzhou, Jiangsu Province, a lantern was lit in the kitchen from the thirteenth until the eighteenth day. The first night was called "trying the lantern;" the last night, "extinguishing the lantern." In Guangdong Province, people donated money to build a shed three or four days before the fifteenth. In the center of the shed, a large lantern of special design was suspended. A stage was built for theatrical performances, which would last for three days and three nights and drew huge audiences. In their houses, people displayed many kinds of lanterns in the shape of fruits and vegetables, figures and birds; some revolved when lit.

At present, while many of the folk customs remain, the superstitions that spawned them have largely been removed. Most lantern festivals are now held in public parks in cities and towns. The lanterns are more varied and colorful, and high technology is used to bring marvelous effects. The themes are both traditional and modern and often take on a local flavor.

The Dragon Boat Festival（端午节）

The Dragon Boat Festival, also called *Duanwu Jie*（端午节）, is another important traditional festival in China.

The Dragon Boat Festival originated in the primitive practice to worship the river god—the dragon. People believed that rivers were controled by dragons who also distributed the rain for farming. Sacrifices were therefore offered to the dragon-king on some day in the fifth lunar month, just before the coming of the rainy season. In so doing, people hoped that the dragon-king would bring them timely rain and let off flood and drought.

The festival is also in memory of the great patriotic poet Qu Yuan（屈原，340 B.C.E.—278 B.C.E.）of the Warring States Period. Qu Yuan was an official of the State of Chu（楚）and served as an adviser of King Huai（reigned from 328 B.C.E.—299 B.C.E.）. At that time the State of Qin（秦）was the strongest and was attempting to annex the other six states. Facing the aggression of Qin, Qu Yuan insisted on an anti-Qin alliance with the other small states but was opposed by other important ministers of the imperial court. Slandered by some treacherous court officials, he was exiled from the court in 286 B.C.E. Thwarted in his ardent ambitions to save his country, he wrote many outstanding poems during his wandering in the vicinity of Dongting Lake（洞庭湖） and the Milo River （汨罗江） in present-day Hunan Province, expressing his ardent love for his homeland and deep sympathy for his people. In the year 278 B.C.E., on hearing that the Qin army had captured the capital of his country, he drowned himself into the Milo River in grief and despair on the fifth day of the fifth lunar month. When the local people heard of his death, they dashed to the river sides to beat gong and drums to scare fishes and dragons away from eating his body and some boatmen raced to the spot to search for him, but in vain. In order to prevent the hungry fishes and dragons from eating, people threw *zongzi*（粽 子, glutinous rice dumplings wrapped in bamboo and reed leaves）, into the river to feed them. It was from these legends that the custom of holding dragon boat races and eating *zongzi* on that day was handed down.

The Mid-Autumn Festival（中秋节）

Falling on the fifteenth day of the eighth month of lunar calendar, the Mid-Autumn Festival, also known as the Moon Festival, is China's second important traditional festival next to the Spring Festival. It is an occasion for family reunion. On this day, the moon is extremely bright and perfectly round. Traditionally, all families would get together on the evening of the festival to have the "family reunion dinner" and eat the round moon-cakes while enjoying the beauty of the full autumn moon. If one of the family members, say, the husband, was far away on duty and could not come home, he would convey his homesickness through the moon to his wife and family; at the same time, his wife and other family members would ask the moon to pass their love, longing and concern to him. So the moon becomes a medium of communication and spiritual sustenance.

There are lots of legends about this festival. The most popular one among the Chinese people is "Houyi shooting the suns"（后羿射日）. The story goes that during the time of Yao（about 2000 B.C.E.）, there lived a talented archer named Houyi. One day ten suns appeared in the sky. Their scorching heat withered the crops on Earth and made people unbearable. Ordered by Emperor Yao, Houyi shot nine of them out of the sky, leaving only one. As a prize for this extraordinary feat, he was given a pill of immortality from a goddess. The pill, however, was stolen by his wife Chang'e（嫦娥） who ate it and flew off to the moon where she lived in solitude, only accompanied by a Jade Rabbit. Later, her husband flew off to dwell on the sun, and so they could see each other once a month, on the fifteenth of every month.

Another legend tells how the custom of eating the moon-cake began. When the first peasant's uprising in 209 B.C.E. was about to break out, the rebels wrote the uprising message on slips of paper and put them in round cakes. When the rebels ate the cake and found the slip of paper, they knew the exact time to take actions.

To the Chinese people today, it is not the romantic stories but the tradition of having family reunion on this festival that has a special appeal. Therefore, the Mid-Autumn Festival will continue to hold a prominent place in China's traditional festivals.

The Qingming（Pure Brightness） Festival（清明节）

Falling on April 4-6 each year, the Qingming Festival is a festival of commemoration. This is the most important day for the Chinese people to hold memorial ceremony.

During the festival, people would go to the cemeteries to offer sacrifices to their ancestors and sweep the tombs of the deceased. After lightly sweeping the tombs, people would offer food, fruits, flowers and favorites with the dead, and then burn incense and paper money and bow before the memorial tablet. In the countryside, the memorial activity would end with the letting out of firecrackers.

The Qingming Festival is also a time for Spring outings, because during this Solar term（节气）, the sun shines brightly, the tree and grass become green and nature is again lively. It is a good time for the city dwellers to go to the suburbs to enjoy the scenery. But in the southern areas of China, it is always rainy at this time of the season. That's why the great poet of the Tang Dynasty, Du Mu, wrote this poem:

It's drizzling during the Qingming time,

Heartbroken the pilgrims are staggering along in a line.

"Where can I find a wineshop" I ask the cowboy,

He points to the apricot village many a mile.

（清明时节雨纷纷, 路上行人欲断魂。

借问酒家何处有, 牧童遥指杏花村。）

The Qingming Festival is a time to plant trees as well, for the survival rate of sapling is high and trees grow fast afterwards. In the past, the Qingming Festival was also called the Arbor Day（植树节）. But since 1979, the Arbor Day has been shifted to March 12, solar calendar.

The Chongyang Festival（重阳节）

The Chongyang Festival, also called the Double Ninth Festival, falls on the 9th day of the 9th lunar month. According to the *Book of Changes*, the number "6" is thought to be *Yin*, meaning feminine, or negative, while the number "9" is *Yang*, meaning masculine, or positive. So the number "9" in both month and day creates Double Ninth Festival, i.e. Chongyang Festival.

Ascending a height is the main activity of the festival. The Chinese believe that ascending a height on that day can avoid epidemics. Therefore the Double Ninth Festival is also called "Height Ascending Festival"（登高节）. Even now, during the festival period people swarm to the mountains — the well-known or little-known. In cities where there are no mountains, a tower or a sky-scraper will do.

People usually eat the *Chongyang Gao*（重阳糕）on that day. In Chinese *Gao*（糕）, meaning cake, has the same pronunciation as height. People do so just to hope for progress in everything they are engaged in. There are no fixed ways to make the cake. Usually, it has nine layers, looking like a tower.

The Double Ninth Festival is also a time when chrysanthemums bloom. The Chinese people have been fond of this kind of flower since ancient times. Enjoying the flourishing chrysanthemum has become a key activity on the festival. Also people will drink chrysanthemum wine and chrysanthemum tea. Women used to stick a chrysanthemum flower into their hair or hang its branches on windows or doors to avoid evil spirits.

The Zhongyuan Festival（中元节）

Similar to the Western Halloween, the Zhongyuan Festival, also called Half July（七月半）, or Ullambana in Buddhism（佛教的盂兰盆节）, is the Ghost Festival in China. It falls on the 15th day of the 7th month of the lunar calendar（in the southern areas of China it is July 14）.

It is believed by the Chinese that the dead become ghosts roaming between Heaven and Earth unless they have descendants to care for them during the Ghost Festival. During this month, the gates of hell are open to free the hungry ghosts who then wander about to seek food on Earth. Some people even think that the ghosts would seek revenge on those who had wronged them in their lives. However, more people remember their ancestors on this day. So the Ghost Festival becomes a festival of filial piety, a time for remembrance of their ancestors. The Chinese avail themselves of the occasion to remember their dead family members and pay tribute to them. They also feel that offering food to the deceased appeases them and wards off bad luck.

Releasing river lanterns（放河灯）is an important activity during the festival. People believe that the river lanterns can comfort and warm the homeless ghosts. They set lotus-flower-shaped lantern on a small paper boat. The lanterns are used to direct the ghosts back to the underground, and when the lanterns drift out of sight, it indicates that the ghosts have already found their way back.

Ullambana was introduced to Japan in the Tang and Sui Dynasties, called O-bon, or simply bon. It has existed in Japan for more than 500 years. It is held from July 13, to welcome O-bon, to July 16 for farewell. O-bon is the Japanese version of the Ghost Festival, which has since been transformed over time into a family reunion holiday during which people return from the big cities to their hometown and visit and clean their ancestors' graves. Traditionally people give gifts to their superiors and acquaintances, too.

Some superstitious beliefs are still prevailing until now. One is that it is bad to go swimming during the 7th month. People think that an evil spirit might make you drown in the water. In addition to this, children are advised to return home early and not to wander around at night, for fear that the wandering ghost might possess them. Usually in the hungry ghost month, no one will get married.

· *Seminar* ·

1. What features of the Spring Festival impress you most?
2. How the custom of holding the dragon boat races and eating *zongzi* on *Duanwu Jie* was formed?

V
Other Traditional Customs

The Twelve Zodiac Animal Sings (十二生肖)

Foreigners often feel interested that Chinese years are named after animals. How did this custom come into being? In ancient times, our ancestor found that signs of the zodiac were twelve in circle. So they used twelve animals to represent the zodiacal signs in the order that: rat, ox, tiger, rabbit, dragon, snake, horse, sheep (or goat), monkey, rooster, dog and pig. This is the twelve zodiac animal signs.

And then how did the order come into being? There are many legends to explain the beginning of the zodiac. One of the most popular explanations reads, in summarized form, as follows: the rat was given the task to invite the animals to report to the Jade Emperor to be selected for the zodiac signs. The cat was a good friend of the rat, but the rat forgot to inform him. So the cat vowed to be the rat's natural enemy for ages to come.

Another most widespread legend goes like this: the Jade Emperor ordered that animals would be designated as calendar signs and the twelve that arrived first would be selected. The night before the event, the cat and his pal, the rat, agreed that the first to wake the following morning would wake up the other. However, the rat broke his promise and arrived at the meeting first. On the way, he encountered the tiger, the ox, the horse, and other animals that ran much faster than he. In order not to fall behind them, the rat jumped on the ox's back. As the ox was happy thinking that he would be the first sign of the years, the rat had already slid in front and became the first lucky animal of the Chinese zodiac. The ox was the second, and then the tiger, the rabbit, the dragon, the snake, the horse, the sheep, the monkey, the rooster, and the dog. The lazy pig finished last. When the cat finally awoke and hurried to the meeting place, it was too late. According to the legend, this is why cats prey on rats.

Based on the order of arrival, the Jade Emperor gave each animal a year of its own, bestowing the nature and characteristics of each animal on people born in the corresponding year.

Traditional Chinese Mascots（中国传统吉祥物）

Loong（龙, dragon）and *Feng*（凤, phoenix）are Chinese traditional mascots, representing people's aspiration to dispel evil spirits and longing for a happy life.

The Chinese dragon is referred to as the divine creature that brings prosperity and good fortune. It is the ultimate representation of the forces of Mother Nature. Many legends drew connection between the dragon and the emperor, and some emperors claimed to have descended from Loong.

The Chinese dragon symbolizes power and excellence, valiancy and boldness, heroism and perseverance, nobility and divinity. It has a head like a camel's, horns like a deer's, eyes like a hare's, ears like a bull's, a neck like a snake's, a belly like a frog's, scales like a carp's, paws like a tiger's, and claws like an eagle's. It lives in the seas, flies up in the sky and coils up in mountains. It can drive out the wandering evil spirits, protect the innocent and bestow safety to people.

Because the Chinese Loong is looked upon as the symbol of good fortune, people have dragon dance to pray for good weather in order to achieve a bumper harvest. Every 2nd of lunar February is the Dragon Raising Head Day（龙抬头日） in China. People would like to have a hair-cut on that day for good luck. In short, the Chinese Loong is an essential symbol of the spirit of China and the Chinese race itself. Dragon pattern is a traditional graphic for the Chinese people with rich cultural connotation and symbolic significance.

The Chinese phoenix is also a Chinese auspicious sign. It exists only in legends and fairy tales. It is used to represent the empress. In Chinese folk lore, phoenix is regarded as the king of hundred birds, predicting luck, expressing love, driving evil, etc. It eats nothing but dewdrops.

The fairy Chinese phoenix has a beak of a rooster, a face of a swallow , a forehead of a fowl, a neck of a snake, a breast of a goose, a back of a tortoise, hindquarters of a stay and a tail of a fish. The phoenix is often depicted in a pair with a male and a female facing each other, symbolizing a duality, the *Yin-Yang*, mutual interdependence in the universe. The male phoenix named *Feng*（凤） is the *Yang* and solar, while the female one *Huang*（凰） is the *Yin* and lunar. The *Feng* and *Huang* together symbolize everlasting love, and as a bridal symbol signifying "inseparable fellowship."

Down the ages, the Chinese *Loong* and the Chinese *Feng* with people's blessing and hope are the symbol of blissful relation between husband and wife, and common metaphor of *Yin* and *Yang*.

Feng Shui（风水）

Feng（凤） means wind in English while *Shui*（水）, water. *Feng Shui* is an ancient Chinese science originating from over 3,000 years ago. At the beginning, it was called *Kan Yu*（堪舆, *Kan* meaning Heaven and *Yu* Earth）, used to monitor the activities of the forces between Heaven and Earth. Ever since the Qing Dynasty, the term *Feng Shui* has been very popular.

Feng Shui is a traditional Chinese discipline which studies the way of co-existence between human beings and the nature. It embodies a simple recognition of the nature by our ancestors. To go into details, *Feng Shui* studies the energy circulation in nature as well as the effect of the living environment on people. The accumulated energy, or *Qi*, though invisible, is everywhere, affecting our existence with its power. On the one hand, it can be particularly positive and beneficial, bringing us luck and wealth; on the other hand, not so positive, conveying hardships.

There are three principles of *Feng Shui*: the unity of human beings with nature, the balance of *Yin* and *Yang*, and the attraction and repulsion of the five elements—metal, wood, water, fire and earth. These principles are set up to help people pursue good fortune and avoid disaster, thus improving the living standard of people. *Feng Shui* is mainly used in community planning and architectural design. It can also be used when there is a change in life goals and a change in family. Nowadays, to improve their quality of life, many people decorate their house according to *Feng Shui* rules.

Two legends are associated with the origin of *Feng Shui*:

Long long ago, a monster appeared in the Yellow River near the town Mengjing（孟津）north of LuoYang（洛阳）. People suffered a lot from it. The land became desolate. And then people turned to Fuxi（伏羲）for help. Fuxi came to the river band with his sword. The monster is no other than the dragon horse（龙马）. On seeing Fuxi, it lay on the ground to beg for mercy. A few days later, the dragon horse carried a jade plate on its back to donate it to Fuxi. On the jade blate, there were some black dots and queer designs. This is *He Tu*（"河图"）, or the River Map. Fuxi studied the River Map and created the Eight Trigrams and wrote the book *I-Ching*.

Another legend goes like this: Yu, the Great（大禹）, was working to control the flood. He opened up the Dragon Gate（龙门）to lead the water of the lake on the south into the Luo River. When the lake was drained, a tortoise, as big as a milestone, appeared in the mud. Yu's man wanted to cut it with his sword but was stopped by Yu. Then, the big tortoise was released into the Luo River. Days after, it carried a shining jade plate and presented it to Yu, the Great. This is *Luo Shu*（《洛书》）, *Book of the Luo River*. There were 65 red characters in it. Yu, the Great examined the red characters time and again, and drew up nine chapters of its contents including calendar, planting, legislation, etc.

He Tu and *Luo Shu* are the foundation of the theory of *Feng Shui*, which are regarded as the good omen predicting peace and harmony of the state, prosperity and wealth of people.

· *Seminar* ·

Search for the legends about the twelve zodiac animal signs and share them in English.

Chapter Seven

Tourism and Culture

- ◆ Culture in Tourism
- ◆ Tourist Resorts and Attractions
- ◆ Tourist Products and Souvenirs

Nowadays tourism becomes the biggest cultural and service industry in the world. With the development of economic globalization and cultural pluralism, tourism is also stepping into the era of globalization.

China is a large country with a long history. Its vast territory affords us a variety of landscapes, numerous scenic spots, and the beauty of nature. Its long history has left us many historical sites and cultural relics. These are abundant resources of tourism.

China has a long history of tourism. Xu Xiake (1586 A.D.— 1641 A.D.) of the Ming Dynasty was the first person who devoted his life to traveling. Within 30 years, he set foot across provinces and regions of today's Jiangsu, Zhejiang, Shandong, Hebei, Shanxi, Shaanxi, Henan, Anhui, Jiangxi, Fujian, Guangdong, Guangxi, Hunan, Hubei, Guizhou and Yunnan. He kept diaries of his observations, and finally combined his travel records into a book—*The Travel Records of Xu Xiake*（《徐霞客游记》）. The book, containing as many as six hundred thousand words, gives a systematic and detailed account of the landscapes and scenic spots, petrographic

Xu Xiake

and topographic features, hydrological and meteorological phenomena, organisms and minerals, local people and their customs. Indeed it is a remarkable work of geography, history and ethnology, whose scientific value has been recognized not only in China but also in the world.

Nowadays tourism has become an industry in China. Many provinces regard it as one of the mainstay of their economy. Every year millions of foreign visitors come to see China and at the same time thousands and thousands of Chinese go abroad for visits and sight-seeing, thus promoting the understanding and cultural exchange of the Chinese people and the peoples of the world.

It is interesting to note that China's tourist emblem has a strong historical flavor—a horse on a mythical "dragon sparrow" against a sky-blue background. The design is based on the famous Han Dynasty bronze horse— "Horse on a Flying Swallow," unearthed in 1969 at Leitai, Wuwei County, Gansu Province, on the Old Silk Road. Studies by experts reveal that the horse is not, as generally believed, the Dawan horse bred in the Dunhuang area, but a divine steed worshipped in the Han Dynasty, and that it rests not on a flying swallow but on a "dragon sparrow," a god of the winds. Zhang Heng (78 A.D.—139 A.D.), a famous Eastern Han Dynasty astronomer and man of letters, refers to these legendary creatures in his *Elegy to the Eastern Capital* as the divine horse traveling through the skies, overriding the dragon sparrow. Thus, the bronze figurine should more appropriately be called "Horse Above Dragon Sparrow." Its use on the emblem suggests that China's tourist industry is soaring towards new heights.

· *Seminar* ·

1. Tell something about the earliest book on tourism in China. What are its contents?

2. Describe China's tourist emblem.

I

Culture in Tourism

Tourism is closely related to culture.

When visiting a place, you are not only interested in its scenery—the beautiful landscape, rivers and mountains, natural surroundings, but also in its people—their life style, their habits and customs, their food and drinks. The educated tourists are most particular about visiting the historic relics—the Great Wall, the Forbidden City, The Ming Tombs, the Qin Shi Huang mausoleum and the great stone Buddha in Leshan, where "the hill is the Buddha while the Buddha is a hill" (山是一尊佛，佛是一座山)．

So cultural tourism becomes a new landmark in the tourist enterprise. For a tourist guide, it is easy to introduce or describe the natural scenery to your guests, for they can see with their own eyes. But it is difficult to explain the culture of a people. You have to study its history, its cultural background, the development of its economy, its mergence and conflict with the culture of other people.

Culture is a complicated subject that covers many grounds. It has rich contents. It is hard to define the word "culture." Some scholars hold that culture includes philosophy, ethics, religion, etc. Others have the opinion that culture is literature and art, science and technology. Still others lay emphasis on social structure and customs of the people.

Culture can be sub-divided into smaller branches. Take Chinese culture for example.

We can sub-group it into China's Tea Culture, China's Wine Culture and China's Culture of Food and Drink, etc. Cultural tourism is a higher stage of tourism. With the development of education, people's interest would turn from going sight-seeing to visiting historical relics, places famous in history or fable.

· Homework ·

Write an article about 800 words on cultural tourism.

II
Tourist Resorts and Attractions

On the land of 960 hundred thousand square kilometers of China, there are lots of tourist resorts and scenic spots. Every province, every county, has its own attractions. Even a thick book can't exhaust them. Here we can only suggest some places in Beijing, Xi'an and Guilin, following the route of Bill Clinton, the 42nd President of the United States, during his visit to China.

In Beijing

Beijing is the Capital of the People's Republic of China. It is also one of the four ancient Chinese capitals. There are many historical relics of the past dynasties in the city.

The Forbidden City（紫禁城）

The Forbidden City, also called the Imperial Palace, was the home of the emperors of the Ming and Qing Dynasties. It is the largest complex of historical buildings. The spacious palace compound, one kilometer from north to south and 750 meters on its east-west axis, is made up of a row of magnificent palaces, characterized by red pillars and yellow tiles. The compound is surrounded by a 50-meter wide moat and a 10-meter high wall and is linked with the rest of the city via four gates. Today the Imperial Palace complex functions as a museum, where one can see a splendid collection of antique porcelains, bronze artifacts and other cultural relics.

Tian'anmen Square（天安门广场）

Tian'anmen Square is one of the largest squares in the world, with the ten-*li*（5 kilometers） Chang'an Street going through. On its west stands the Great Hall of the People, and on its east the Museum of Chinese Revolution. Its front is the magnificent Tiananmen castle, the south entrance to the Imperial Palace, on which Chairman Mao Zedong proclaimed the founding of the People's Republic of China on October 1, 1949. South of the square is the Mausoleum of Chairman Mao Zedong.

Temple of Heaven（天坛）

Situated on the east of Qianmen Street, the Temple of Heaven is a quiet place. There are three structures: the Hall of Prayer for Good Harvest（祈年殿）, the Circular Mount Altar（环丘坛）and the Imperial Vault of Heaven（皇穹宇）.

The Summer Palace（颐和园）

Located in the hilly country some 13 kilometers to the northwest of Beijing, the Summer Palace was built by the Qing Empress Dowager（慈禧太后）. Many magnificent buildings are scattered between Lake Kun Ming（昆明湖）and the Longevity Hill（万寿山）. They are linked by the 700-meter Long Corridor. The yellow

and blue tiles and vermilion pillars form beautiful reflections in the lake. The Tower of Buddhist Incense（佛香阁）, on the summit of the Longevity Hill is a large octagonal building standing on a 60-meter marble base, and forms the pivot of the 290 hectares area of the Summer Palace ground.

The Ming Tombs（十三陵）

The Ming Tombs are located at the foot of the Tian Shou Hills about 40 kilometers northwest of Beijing. Scattered around are the tombs of thirteen Ming emperors. The Sacred Way is lined on both sides with stone statues of warriors, elephants, camels, lions and other animals. The palaces, gardens and tombs were built on a huge scale in a spacious basin area about 40 kilometers wide. One of the tombs has been excavated and opened to tourists.

The Great Wall (长城)

The Great Wall was built during the Warring States Period to prevent invasions by the nomadic nations from the north. It was completed by the first Qin emperor who united China into one country at that time. The first Qin emperor mobilized several hundred thousand builders to link sections of the previous walls, thus completing what is known today as the Great Wall of China. The wall is 6,700 kilometers long from Shanhaiguan, which overlooks the gulf of Bo Hai, to Jiayuguan Pass in Gansu Province. The average height of the wall is 7.8 meters, and its width averages 6.5 meters at the base and 5.8 meters at the top. Rectangular lookout posts were built about every 100 meters.

The section of the Great Wall frequented by tourists is in Badaling, 75 kilometers to the north of Beijing.

In Xi'an

Xi'an was the capital of 11 dynasties, China's political, economic and cultural center from the 11th century B.C.E. to the 10th century A.D. Called Chang'an during the Tang period, it was the terminal of the Silk Road, a cosmopolitan city ranking with Rome.

Places of interest within the city include the 64-meter Dayan (Big Wild Goose) Pagoda (大雁塔), where the great monk scholar Xuan Zang lived and translated the Buddhist scriptures after his return from India; and the Shaanxi Provincial Museum, which houses 30,000 artifacts and ancient relics. Located in the suburbs is Qin Shihuang Mausoleum (秦始皇陵), which was built for the first emperor of the Qin Dynasty. About 8,000 life-size terra cotta of soldiers and horses were buried here to protect the emperor after his death. The unearthed part of the

mausoleum has been turned into a museum. There are many other places to visit, such as Huaqing Springs (华清池), famous for the romance between Emperor Xuan Zong and his concubine Yang Guifei of the Tang Dynasty; and the tombs of the third and fourth Tang emperors, where over 120 stone statues of men and animals line a 500-meter access road.

In Guilin

Situated in South China, Guilin is like a glittering pearl on an evergreen carpet. With green hills, limpid waters, fantastic caves and stately rocks, the scenery there enjoys the eulogy of "topping all under heaven." The name of the city is derived from the cassia tree called "Gui" in Chinese, and even today the cassia trees lining the streets of the town are covered with golden yellow flowers in autumn, filling the air with sweet-sour scent.

The section of the town adjoining the Li Jiang River (漓江) is a marvelous sight. The beautiful mountains, trees and lights are reflected in the limpid water, creating scenes unparalleled in the world and looking exactly like a scroll painting of a Chinese landscape. Other places of interest include the Solitary Beauty Peak, the Reed Flute Cave, and Mount Elephant. A cruise down the Li Jiang River to Yangshuo is indispensable for tourists.

The Solitary Beauty Peak (*Duxiufeng*, 独秀峰) is located in the center of the city. This famous peak looks out over the west bank of the Li Jiang River. Following the winding path of over 200 steps, you can reach the pinnacle where you can enjoy a *panorama* of the city and other peaks.

The Reed Flute Cave (*Ludiyan*, 芦笛岩) is situated on the banks of the Peach Flower Stream (*Taohuajiang*, 桃花江), about seven kilometers northwest of the city. Under the hill there is a limestone cave over two kilometers long. The milky stalagmites and stalactites are illuminated with various types of light, creating fantastic sights.

Mount Elephant (*Xiangbishan*, 象鼻山) is a rock formation which resembles an elephant with its trunk in the water. It is located in the south of the city on the bank of the Li Jiang River. On its summit is a pagoda built during the Ming Dynasty. This is a vantage point where tourists can have a bird's-eye view of the city. Another vantage point with a superb view is on the  Diecai Hill (叠彩山) where poems by generations of poets since the Tang Dynasty have been inscribed on the cliffs.

A cruise down the Li Jiang River from Guilin to Yangshuo is the most exciting experience of your visit to Guilin. People say that "the scenery in Guilin is unparallel in

the world," yet there is another saying that "the mountains and waters in Yangshuo are even better than those in Guilin." As the boat proceeds along the river, a variety of scenes is unfolded on each bank. Here and there rock pinnacles are wreathed in the mist. Between the various rock formations, villages are blent with bamboo groves. The boat leaves Guilin in the morning and arrives at the town of Yangshuo in the afternoon. This is a stretch of scenery which might have been lifted straight out of a Chinese landscape painting. After the cruise, passengers can either put up in Yangshuo or return to Guilin in an hour by bus.

Some Famous Grottoes and Mountains in China

Longmen Grottoes（龙门石窟）

Located 12 kilometers to the south of Luoyang City, Henan Province, the Longmen Grottoes are on the rocky cliffs on both banks of the Yishui River, measuring 1,000 meters from north to south.

The carvings of the grottoes began in 494 A.D., in the Northern Wei Dynasty. Large-scale work was done over a period of 400 years in the Eastern Wei, Western Wei, Northern Qi, Northern Zhou, Sui and Tang Dynasties. According to investigations made after 1949, there are 1,325 caves, 750 niches and over 40 pagodas of various sizes, with a total of more than 100,000 statues of Buddhist images ranging in size from only 2 centimeters to 17.14 meters.

The Longmen Grottoes display great richness and variety. The fine artistic technique of the carvings and the vividness and diversity of form and expression of the figures make the grottoes a treasure-house for studying China's history of sculptural art.

Mogao Grottoes in Dunhuang（敦煌莫高窟）

The Mogao Grottoes lie about 25 kilometers from the county seat of Dunhuang in Gansu Province. There are 1,000 Buddha caves in Dunhuang containing pictures of the world's finest art. They were cut out in the steep cliff at the foot of the Mingshan Mountain. Today, over 492 caves still remain.

The most important cave is the preserving Buddhist

Scriptures Cave. Many caves have stories. One of the most famous is outlined in a series of pictures about a woman who was badly treated by her husband. While returning to her mother, she encountered a wolf that killed her two children, one of them newly born. After becoming a nun, she learned that her current miseries were a punishment for mistreating her stepsister in a previous incarnation.

Beginning in the fourth century, these grottoes were sacred places for Buddhist pilgrims. They were created over a period of a thousand years. The grottoes give a graphic picture in art form of the life and activity of the people of those early times.

Yungang Caves（云冈石窟）

The cave temples of Yungang are situated in the north cliff of the Wuzhou Mountain, about 16 kilometers outside Datong City, Shanxi Province. There are 53 Buddhist cave temples, most of which were cut out of the rock between 453 A.D. to 459 A.D. , when the town was the capital of the Northern Wei Dynasty. They contain 51,000 statues and constitute one of the largest groups of stone cave temples in China. It is a much smaller site than Dunhuang and Longmen, but it contains much fine Northern Wei sculpture.

The caves are dominated by a 17-meter-high massive statue of the historical Buddha, Sakyamuni, with huge shoulders corresponding with descriptions of the Buddha in the scriptures.

Huashan（华山）

Huashan was recognized as one of the five great mountains in China two thousand years ago. It rises 2,100 meters above the confluence of three important rivers, the Luo, the Wei and the Yellow River. One hundred and twenty kilometers east of Xi'an City, Huashan was formerly worshipped by the Taoists. Pilgrims, poets, painters and tourists used to come to see its magnificent scenery of sheer peaks and precipices, waterfalls, springs and pine trees, as well as mountain slopes dotted with old Taoist temples and monasteries. Huashan is not an easy ascent. In front of one particularly steep path called the "Monkey's Frown" are two words carved into the rock: "Turn back!"

Huangshan（黄山）

Situated in the southern Anhui Province, the 1,680-meter-high Huangshan is one of China's best-known scenic spots, famous for its spectacular rocky peaks, odd-shaped pines, crystal-clear springs and seas of clouds.

Huangshan consists of 72 peaks, of which the most famous are: Lotus Flower Peak, Bright Summit and Heavenly Capital. The granite summits are accessible by walking trails, dotted with pavilions, temples and guesthouses.

Songshan（嵩山）

Located in Dengfeng County, Henan Province, the Songshan Mountain rises 1,500 meters. The top of the mountain offers a magnificent view of the 72 peaks of Songshan all round, the vast expanse of the fertile central plain below, with the Temple of

Songshan, the Temple of the Central Mountain and Gaocheng Observatory in view.

Taishan（泰山）

Taishan (or Mt. Tai) ranks first of the five sacred mountains in China. Towering 1,540 meters above sea level, Mt. Tai is a symbol of loftiness and grandeur. It was the mountain chosen by emperors as the site of imperial sacrifices to Heaven. Visitors will expect a strenuous climb up the precipitous paths and flights of stone steps which wind through pine-clad slopes.

At the summit are the guesthouse and the main temple of the Princess of the Colored Clouds. The princess is a cult figure among the peasant women of Shandong Province. Today visitors enjoy the climb in the hope they will have a glimpse of the often elusive but magnificent sunrise when the sun appears like a ball of fire from a sea of clouds.

· *Seminar* ·

Describe one of the tourist resorts and attractions in China.

Ⅲ
Tourist Products and Souvenirs

China offers countless tourist souvenirs which remind one of its long history and the traditions of its people. Among them are handicrafts, such as porcelain, jade and cloisonné, carved lacquer ware, paper-cuts, filigree, carpets, lanterns, fans, flowers made of satin or silk, animals, birds and flowers made of colored glass, figurines of painted clay, etc. and many other quality products such as jewelry, calligraphy and paintings, materials for seal, ink stones, ink slabs, liquor, tea and Chinese medicine.

Porcelain

China was the first to manufacture true porcelain, as suggested by its name, china. Seven or eight thousand years ago during the new stone age, the inhabitants of the Huanghe River (Yellow River) basin began to make pottery. The exact date of the first true porcelain is difficult to fix, but large quantities of unearthed vessels show that by the time of the Shang Dynasty, vitreous glazes had come into use. According to chemical analyses, the black glazed ceramic ware of this period possesses some of the characteristics of porcelain and is the forerunner of the green and blue porcelain ware of later periods. Primitive porcelain developed gradually and did not attain a high level of artistic maturity until the Eastern Han Dynasty when pottery firing and glazing techniques had reached a very high level and fine pottery-ware was beginning to appear. The quality of the porcelain-ware produced in this period was extremely fine, with thick and even glazes. Modern analysis reveals the perfect fusion of the body. The degree of absorbency and hardness of the body as well as the fusion of the glazes are all up to present-day standards.

The Tang and Song Dynasties were a time of rapid development in porcelain manufacture. During the Tang Dynasty, the light green *yue*（悦）ware produced in Shaoxing, Zhejiang Province in the south, and the white *xing*（荣）ware produced in Meiqiu, Hebei Province in the north were outstanding. The Song porcelain-ware had more pleasing colors and shapes. There were five major kilns, each producing porcelain with distinguished style: white *ding*（定）ware; powdery blue *ru*（汝）ware; the "purple mouth and iron foot" ware of the *guan*（官）or official kiln; *ge*（哥）ware with its crackled surface; and the *jun*（均）ware with its color trans（转移）mutations（变化）taking place during firing.

Porcelain manufacture reached its height of excellence in the Ming and Qing

Dynasties. The Ming and Qing porcelain-ware, such as the polychrome and blue and white bowls, jugs and vases, are even better known today. During these dynasties almost the entire porcelain industry was concentrated in Jingdezhen(景德镇), Jiangxi Province. In the Ming Dynasty, porcelain painted in cobalt oxide under a glaze became the most famous and was shipped in large quantities to the Middle and Near East. As a matter of fact, porcelain made in Jingdezhen began to find its way to Europe from the 17th century onwards and can now be seen in many large English collections. Among the most famous types of porcelain during the Ming and Qing are famille rose(红釉), blue and white *doucai*(斗彩, contending colors), sacrificial red, rouge(胭脂) ware and misty blue eggshell porcelain.

Jade

For several thousand years, the carving of jade has been an intrinsic part of Chinese culture; and that may be one of the reasons why Chinese jade is renowned throughout the world.

The Chinese people's love and use of jade dates back to the Shang Dynasty when jade was used as a medium of exchange. To the ancient Chinese, jade was the most precious stones, a sacred material containing the quintessence of virtue. In early times, the use of jade was confined to ritual purposes, but it gradually came to be adapted for purely ornamental objects such as jewelry, dress accessories and items of personal adornment. In imperial times, jade was regarded as a symbol of wealth and rank. Chinese emperors carried a scepter of jade which was seen as proof of their mandate from Heaven. Imperial documents were stamped with a jade seal, and amulets of jade were worn by officials at the imperial court as an indication of their rank and power.

Legend has it that the Chinese people believe that jade transmits its superior qualities to those who wear it. In fact, most Chinese wear a piece of jade as jade is believed to ward off evil forces and protect the wearer against misfortune. For this reason, jade bracelets are auspicious gifts for infants, and older people often wear a talisman of jade—the theory being that if a person falls, the jade will break but not the wearer.

Chinese jade appears in nature in a great variety of ways. The jade carving industry in China now uses 30 types of jade and precious stones. These include nephrite(which itself encompasses white jade, green jade, black jade and jasper), jadeite, lapis lazuli, turquoise, agate and malachite. The majority of Chinese jade is used to make jade articles and objects, with small amounts of finest quality jade set aside for jewelry manufacture. According to historical records, jade is found in more than 100 different locations in China. Nephrite, the traditional favorite of Chinese artisans, is quarried both in Fengtian district of Taiwan and in the Xinjiang Urgur Autonomous Region.

Jade-carving is one of the highest achievements of Chinese craftsmanship. In medieval China, jade was much revered and used as ritual objects notably for Buddhist figurines. Later with the development of jade-carving technique, more beautiful and complicated jade articles could be carved and people began to use them as jewelry and ornaments or as decorations and objects for collection because of its antiquarian associations.

One of the greatest extant jade-carving pieces is "Great Yu Controlling Waters" (大禹治水), which is called the "king of jade." This huge jade object, nearly two meters in height and over 5,000 kilograms in weight, now displayed in the Palace Museum, was carved in the Qing Dynasty out of Hetian nephrite in Xinjiang Province, one of the most famous kinds of jade in China.

Cloisonné (景泰蓝)

Cloisonné is a traditional enamelware (上釉瓷器), known as "Jingtai Blue" in China, with a history of over 500 years. It is so called because "blue" was the typical color used for enameling and "Jingtai" was the title of the Ming emperor's reign. There is a great variety of products, such as the traditional vases, jars, bowls, boxes and ash-trays. Brilliant in color and splendid in design, they enjoy a high reputation both at home and abroad.

The making of cloisonne is rather complicated. The process begins with the casting of bronze into different shapes—vases, bowls and the like, to which flat bronze wires are then affixed in decorative patterns. Enamels of different colors are applied to fill the cloisons or hollows. Each cloisonné piece is fired three times with a fresh coat of enamel each time. After firing, the pieces are ground and polished, and look to be gilded.

Techniques of wire filigree in cloisonné production were very sophisticated by the time of Qianlong in the Qing Dynasty, and a variety of patterns of great subtlety and grace were used. Chinese cloisonné was introduced to the Western market in the last years of the Qing Dynasty, and in 1904 it received a first prize at the Chicago World Fair.

Since 1949, cloisonné craftsmanship has undergone great development in two respects. First, the color range of enamels has been extended to pea green, rose purple, coffee, egg yellow, azure and gold. Most cloisonné pieces now are made with polychrome, and polished to create various tones. Secondly, the designs have been improved by borrowing from patterns found on old silks.

Embroidery

Embroidery is a traditional craft in China. In ancient times, girls in towns and cities learnd this art at an early age, which would give them an advantage when they were going to marry. The embroidery unearthed in 1958 in a tomb of the Warring States Period in Changsha, Hunan Province, testifies to the age of this folk art. The unearthed embroidery, a dragon and a phoenix design on closely woven silk, shows a fairly high level of craftsmanship. The stitches are neat, the needlecraft delicate and the design lively.

Embroidery was first developed by local women to decorate their skirts, pouches and other articles. With its designs rich in life and full of colors, it has gradually developed into a national art. There are four famous embroideries in China, namely Xiang embroidery(湘绣, produced in Hunan Province), Su embroidery (苏绣, produced in Suzhou, Zhejiang Province), Yue embroidery(粤绣, produced in Guangdong Province) and Shu embroidery(蜀绣, produced in Sichuan Province), each with its own style.

Early embroidery had the design and patterns only on one side, while the reverse side had irregular stitches and thread ends. Later the technique of double-sided embroidery evolved. Both sides of embroidery display the same design in the same color. In the 1950s, double-sided embroidery of a new technique enabled the two sides of the embroidery to have the same design but in different colors. A peony design, for instance, would be red on one side and yellow on the other.

However, the diligent artists continued their efforts to improve the technique. In 1980, a new breakthrough was made in Hunan Province—double-sided embroidery with different designs and colors. This wonderful work of art brought Xiang embroidery to a new peak.

In 1983, a double-sided embroidery, 1.06 meters high and 4.01 meters wide, named "The Enchanting Scenery of Dongting Lake" was produced by the Hunan Embroidery

Research Institute. In the process of creation, about 8 stitching methods and a dozen kinds of multi-colored silk threads were used. The whole work took 20 embroiderers more than 3,000 workdays to finish. The embroidery is now displayed in the Hunan Section of the Great Hall of the People, adding new splendor to both Xiang embroidery and the Great Hall of the People.

Silk

Silk is one of China's contributions to the world's civilization. China was the first in the world to manufacture and use silk. According to legend, Lei Zu（嫘祖）, wife of the mythical Yellow Emperor, taught the Chinese people the art of sericulture.

During the Shang Dynasty, there were already government-sponsored silk production workshops. By the time of the Zhou Dynasty, the production of silk had spread as far as the Hanshui River（汉水）, the Yellow River and the Changjiang River valleys. The Chinese were producing splendid silks with subtle designs woven into the fabric as well as silk decorated with colored embroidery. By the time of the Spring and Autumn and Warring States Periods, silk had been manufactured throughout China. Considerable progress had been made in weaving and dyeing techniques.

During the Tang Dynasty, further advances were made in silk manufacturing, resulting in even more delicate and exquisite products. During the Qing Dynasty, silk production greatly increased, and the silk of Zhejiang Province enjoyed an especially high reputation.

Since ancient times, silk has been one of China's traditional exports. Chinese fine silks were exported during the Western Han Dynasty in the second century B.C.E. A portion of the exports was carried on camel backs along the famous caravan route known as the "Silk Road" to the Middle East, eventually reaching Western Europe.

So far as texture and workmanship are concerned, there are four kinds of Chinese silk which can be ranged as the finest and best-known. They are made respectively in Jiangsu, Hunan, Sichuan and Guangdong provinces. After thousands of years of development and influenced by geographical conditions, local customs, art and culture, each of these silks has evolved a style of its own and has some special characteristics; some favor fine composition, bright color and great variety; and some lay stress on naturalness and follow the principle that the silk thread should go with the growth or development of the things or animals to be embroidered.

China currently produces several hundred varieties of silk in thousands of colors and designs, such as one-side embroidery, double-sided embroidery, "three differences"

（double-face with different colors, different designs and different embroidering methods）, and other practical things like the quilt-cover, pillow-case, table cloth, cloth and shoes. These beautiful silk products have found ready markets in more than 100 countries and regions in the world. With its unique texture, exquisite skill, and strong national style, Chinese silk has won the love of more and more people throughout the world.

· *Seminar* ·

Describe one of the Chinese tourist products and souvenirs.

General Review

Chapter One

1. Why do the Chinese Han people usually call themselves "the descendants of Yan and Huang"?

2. Why was China called "the Middle Kingdom"?

3. Tell the stories about Yao, Shun, Yu.

4. Tell the story of "tear bamboo".

5. Tell the story of old Master Jiang.

6. Which is the turning point in Chinese history which marked the close of ancient Chinese period and the beginning of modern history?

Chapter Two

1. What are Four Books and Five Classics?

2. What is the central doctrine of Confucius?

3. According to Dr. Sun Yan-sen, what is the Chinese spirit?

4. Tell a story about Mencius.

5. The Taoist philosophy may be summed up in two points. What are they?

6. What are the Buddhist Three Doctrines and Four Noble Truths?

7. What is the core of Moism?

8. What is the central doctrine of Legalism?

9. What is the philosophy underlying the book *I-Ching*?

Chapter Three

1. Describe the four major books of Pre-Qin Literature.

2. What is *Yuefu*?

3. What is China's first book on literary criticism? Tell its main contents.

4. Introduce the three great poets of the Tang Dynasty: Li Bai, Du Fu and Bai Juyi.

5. What is *Ci*? Can you tell some famous *Ci* poets?

6. What is *Zaju*? Describe some *Zaju* plays.

7. What are the four great novels of the Ming and Qing Dynasties?

8. What are the Six Arts and the Four Treasures of the Studio in ancient China?

9. How did the Chinese calligraphy come into being?

10. What is the theory of *Xieyi*—painting the feeling in traditional Chinese painting?

11. What are the general principles of *Qigong*?

12. Describe the facial patterns and costumes of Beijing Opera.

Chapter Four

1. What are the Four Great Inventions in ancient China?

2. Tell the story how gunpowder was invented.

3. Which is the earliest medical classic in China?

4. Which book in ancient China comprises 1897 varieties of medicines grouped under 60 categories?

5. Which book is the first complete and systematic book on agriculture in the history of mankind?

6. Tell briefly the contents of the book *Work of Nature and Exploitation of Things*.

Chapter Five

1. What is *Sixue* in ancient China?

2. Give a brief account of the present educational system of China.

3. Comment on the curriculum of nine-year compulsory education.

4. Comment on the civil service examination.

5. Can you give more details about the five types of higher learning besides the regular universities and colleges in China: correspondence, evening school, TV university, vocational college and self-taught programs?

Chapter Six

1. Which is the earliest tea classic in China?

2. Tell a story about Shennong.

3. Tell a ghost story described in Liu Jingshu's *Fantastic Garden*.

4. According to the ways of manufacturing, how many kinds can Chinese tea be divided into?

5. What is the difference between the Green Tea and the Black Tea?

6. According to the brewing process, how many kinds can the Chinese wines be classified into?

7. How does Maotai get its brand mark?

8. What are the four major schools of cooking in China? Describe them in details.

9. How did holding dragon boat race and eating *zongzi* on the Dragon Boat Festival become a custom?

Chapter Seven

1. What is the first book describing tourism in China? What are its contents?

2. Explain China's tourist emblem.

3. Describe one or two of Chinese tourist resorts and attractions.

4. Describe one or two of Chinese tourist products and souvenirs.

5. What are the four famous embroideries in China?

Appendix

Selected Chinese Historical and Cultural Classics
（中国历代文化典籍选）

一、思想、政治典籍

《十三经》 *The Thirteen Classics*　　《论语》 *The Confucian Analects*

《中庸》 *The Doctrine of Mean*　　《孟子》 *Mencius*

《易经》 *I-Ching*　　《礼记》 *Book of Rites*

《鹖冠子》 *He Guan Zi*　　《慎子》 *Shen Zi*

《荀子》 *XunZi*　　《列子》 *Lie Zi*

《老子》 *Lao Zi*　　《庄子》 *Zhuang Zi*

《韩非子》 *Han FeiZi*　　《管子》 *Guan Zi*

《墨子》 *Mo Zi*　　《盐铁论》 *Argument on Salt and Iron*

《抱朴子》 *Bao Pu Zi*

《颜氏家训》 *Yan's Admonitions to His Descendants*

《商君书》 *Book of Shang Yang*　　《吕氏春秋》 *Lv's Spring and Autumn Annals*

《新语》 *The New Remarks*　　《新书》 *The New Book*

《弘明集》 *The Hongming Collection*

《广弘明集》 *The Grand Hongming Collection*

《符子》 *Fu Zi*

《春秋繁露》 *Collected Notes on Spring and Autumn*

《淮南子》 *Writings of Prince Huainan*

《二程全书》 *The Chengs' Collections*

《四书集注》 *Collected Annotations of the Four Books*

《焚书》 *The Burning of Books*　　《续焚书》 *Burning of Books (Continued)*

《明夷待访录》 *MingyiDaifang Lu*　　《日知录》 Daily Additions to Knowledge

《传习录》 *Chuan Xi Records*

《曾国藩家书》 *Selected Letters of Zeng Guofan*

《临川集》 *The Linchuan Collections*

《资政新篇》 *New Guide to Government*

《大同书》 *Great Harmony*

二、史学典籍

《尚书》 *Book of History*　　　《春秋》 *Spring and Autumn Annals*

《左传》 *ZuoZhuan*　　　　　　《国语》 *Remarks of States*

《战国策》 *Zhan Guo Ce*　　　《史记》 *Historical Records*

《汉书》 *Book of Han*　　　　《三国志》 *History of the Three Kingdoms*

《后汉书》 *Book of the Posterior Han Dynasty*

《史通》 *A Great History*　　　《贞观政要》 *The Political Program of Zhen Guan*

《资治通鉴》 *ZizhiTongjian*　　《读通鉴论》 *Comment on History*

三、文学作品

《诗经》 *Book of Songs*　　　《晏子春秋》 *The Years of Yan Zi*

《楚辞》 *Chuci*　　　　　　　《新序》 *New Order*

《说苑》 *Forum*　　　　　　　《嵇康集》 *An Anthology of Jikang*

《曹操集》 *An Anthology of Cao Cao*　《笑林》 *The Joke Forest*

《博物志》 *Records of Myriad Things*　《搜神记》 *Stories of Immortals*

《世说新语》 *New Talks on Old Farces*

《陶渊明集》 *Collected Works of Tao Yuanming*

《文选》 *Selected Writings*

《全唐诗》 *A Complete Collection of Tang Poetry*

《大唐西域记》 *Travels to the West*

《骆宾王集》 *Collected Works of Luo Binwang*

《陈子昂集》 *Collected Works of Chen Zi'ang*

《王昌龄集》 *Collected Works of Wang Changling*

《王右丞集》 *Collected Works of Prime Minister Wang*

《李太白集》 *Collected Works of Li Taibai*

《杜工部集》 *Collected Works of Du Fu*

《白香山集》 *Collected Works of Bai Xiangshan*

《孟东野诗集》 *Collected Works of MengDongye*

《柳河东集》 *Collected Works of Liu Hedong*

《金奁集》 *A Book of Gold Dressing-box*

《欧阳修全集》 *Collected Works of Ouyang Xiu*

《苏东坡集》 *Collected Works of Su Dongpo*

《乐章集》 *A Collection of Movements*　　《片玉集》 *A Collection of Jade Fragments*

《李清照集》 *A Collection of Li Qingzhao's Works*

《陆游集》 *Collected Works of Lu You*　　《稼轩长短句》 *The Poetry of Jiaxuan*

《太平广记》 *Extensive Records of Taiping*

《雁门集》 *The Yanmen Collection*

《关汉卿戏曲集》 *Collected Works of Guan Hanqing*

《西厢记》 *The Romance of the Western Chamber*

《乐府诗集》 *A Collection of Yuefu Poems*

《水浒传》 *Outlaws of the Marsh*

《三国演义》 *The Romance of the Three Kingdoms*

《西游记》 *The Pilgrimage to the West*

《牡丹亭》 *The Peony Pavilion*

《三言》 *San Yan*　　　　　　　《二拍》 *ErPai*

《聊斋志异》 *Strange Stories from the Liaozhai Studio*

《长生殿》 *The Palace of Eternal Youth*

《桃花扇》 *The Peach Blossom Fan*

《儒林外史》 *The Scholars*　　　《红楼梦》 *A Dream of Red Mansions*

《镜花缘》 *Flowers in a Mirror*　　《浮生六记》 *Six Chapters of a Floating Life*

《龚定庵诗集》 *Collected Poems of Gong Ding'an*

《老残游记》 *The Travel Records of Lao Can*

《官场现形记》 *The True Colors of Officialdom*

《宋元戏曲史》 *History of the Traditional Dramas and Operas in the Song and Yuan Dynasties*

《清代学术概论》 *An Outline of Learning in the Qing Dynasty*

《太平天国文选》 *Selected Works of the Taiping Heavenly Kingdom*

《五四运动文选》 *Selected Works of the May 4th Movement*

《鲁迅杂感选集》 *Selected Essays of Lu Xun*

《布碌陀》 *Bulutuo*　　　　　《鲁般鲁饶》 *Lu Ban Lu Rao*

《打歌·创世纪》 *Song of the Creation of the World*

《安王和祖王》 *King An and KingZu*　《摆手歌》 *The Songs of Waving Hands*

《江格尔》 *Jiangle*　　　　　　《玛纳斯》 *Manas*

《珠郎娘美》 *Zhulang and Niangmei*　《梅葛》 *Mei Ge*

《盘古大歌》 *King Pan's Songs*　　《古史歌》 *The Song of Ancient History*

《格萨尔王传》 *King Gesar*

四、文学评论典籍

《文心雕龙》 *Literary Mind and Carving of Dragons*

《诗品》 *Appreciation of Poetry*

《彝族诗论》 *Critique on Poetry of the Yi Nationality*

《沧浪诗话》 *Canglang Notes on Poets and Poetry*

《论傣族诗歌》 *Poetry of the Dai Nationality*

《闲情偶寄》 *Unexpected Gains in Leisure*

五、科学和技术典籍

《孙子兵法》 *Art of War*

《九章算术》 *The Nine-Chapter Arithmetic*

《黄帝内经》 *The Yellow Emperor's Internal Classic*

《水经注》 *Annotations to Book of Watercourses*

《齐名要术》 *Important Arts for Agriculture*

《梦溪笔谈》 *Sketches in Mengxi Garden*

《本草纲目》 *Compendium of MateriaMedica*

《农政全书》 *A Complete Book for Agriculture*

《天工开物》 *Work of Nature and Exploitation of Things*

《徐霞客游记》 *The Travel Records of Xu Xiake*

《茶经》 *Tea Classics*

《陶说》 *On Ceramics*

六、语言文字典籍

《尔雅》 *ErYa*

《方言》 *Dialects*

《说文解字》 *Analytical Dictionary of Chinese Characters*

《马氏文通》 *Ma's Grammar*

七、综合类典籍

《山海经》 *Book of the Mountains and Seas*

《东巴经》 *The Dongba Scripture*

《太平御览》 *Taiping Yulan*

《三字经》 *The Three-Word Cannon*

《增广贤文》 *The Eye-Opening Book*

《古文观止》 *GuwenGuanzhi*

《四库全书》 *SikuQuanshu*

Bibliography

Kerson & Rosemary Huang. *I-Ching* [M]. New York: Workman Publishing Company, Inc., 1987.

Qi Wen. *China—A General Survey* [M]. Bei Jing: Foreign Languages Press, 1979.

Wm. Theodore De Bary, Wing-Tsit Chan & Burton Watson. *Sources of Chinese Tradition* [M]. New York: Columbia University Press, 1960.

Zhou Yi & Liang Yihua. *Chinese Culture* [M]. Gui Lin: Guangxi Education Press, 1993.

程爱民 . *Aspects of Chinese Culture* [M]. 南京: 译林出版社 ,1994.

常俊跃 , 霍跃红 , 王焱 , 赵永青 . 中国文化（英文版）[M]. 2 版 . 北京: 北京大学出版社 , 2016.

刘城淮 , 李全华 , 王朋 . 中华古典名著精解 [M]. 长沙: 中南工业大学出版社 , 1993.

汤恩佳 , 朱仁夫 . 孔子读本 [M]. 广州: 南方日报出版社 , 2007.

薛荣 . 中国文化教程（英文版修订本）[M]. 南京: 南京大学出版社 , 2014.

訾缨 , 朱红梅 . 中国古代社会与文化英文教程 [M]. 2 版 . 北京: 北京大学出版社 , 2015.

张丹子 , 胡曙中 . 旅游接待英语 [M]. 上海: 上海外语教育出版社 , 1987.

中国社科院 . 中国文学史 [M]. 北京: 人民文学出版社 , 1962.

朱岐新 , 张秀桂 . 中国文化集锦 [M]. 北京: 旅游教育出版社 , 1994.

周仪 . 中国文化故事（英汉对照）[M]. 上海: 同济大学出版社 , 2012.

周仪 , 罗平 . 中国古代格言妙语英译 [M]. 南宁: 广西教育出版社 ,1998.

周仪 , 赵勇 , 罗家如 . 中国历代文化典籍概要 [M]. 北京: 世界图书出版公司 , 2000.